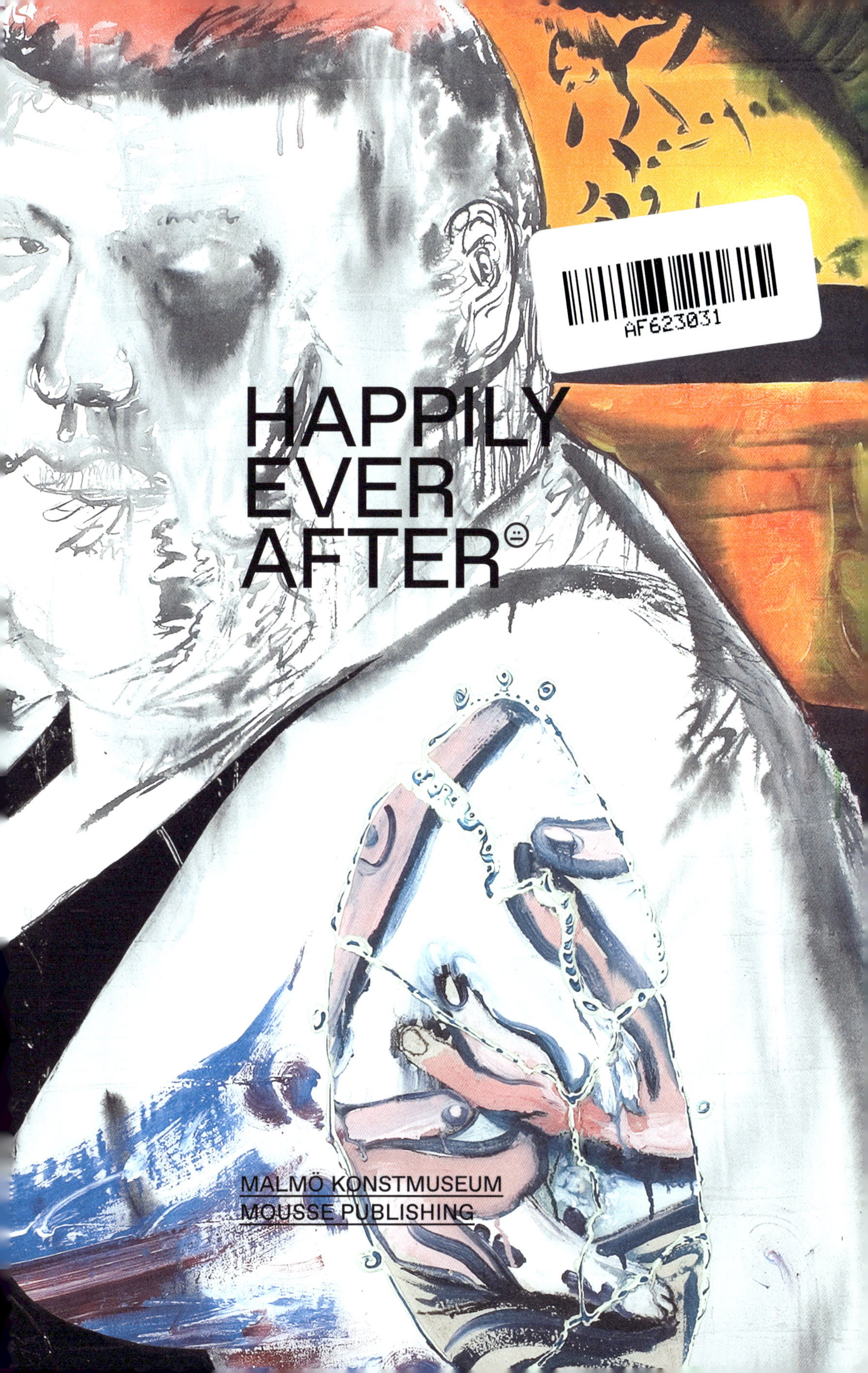

HAPPILY EVER AFTER☺

MALMÖ KONSTMUSEUM
MOUSSE PUBLISHING

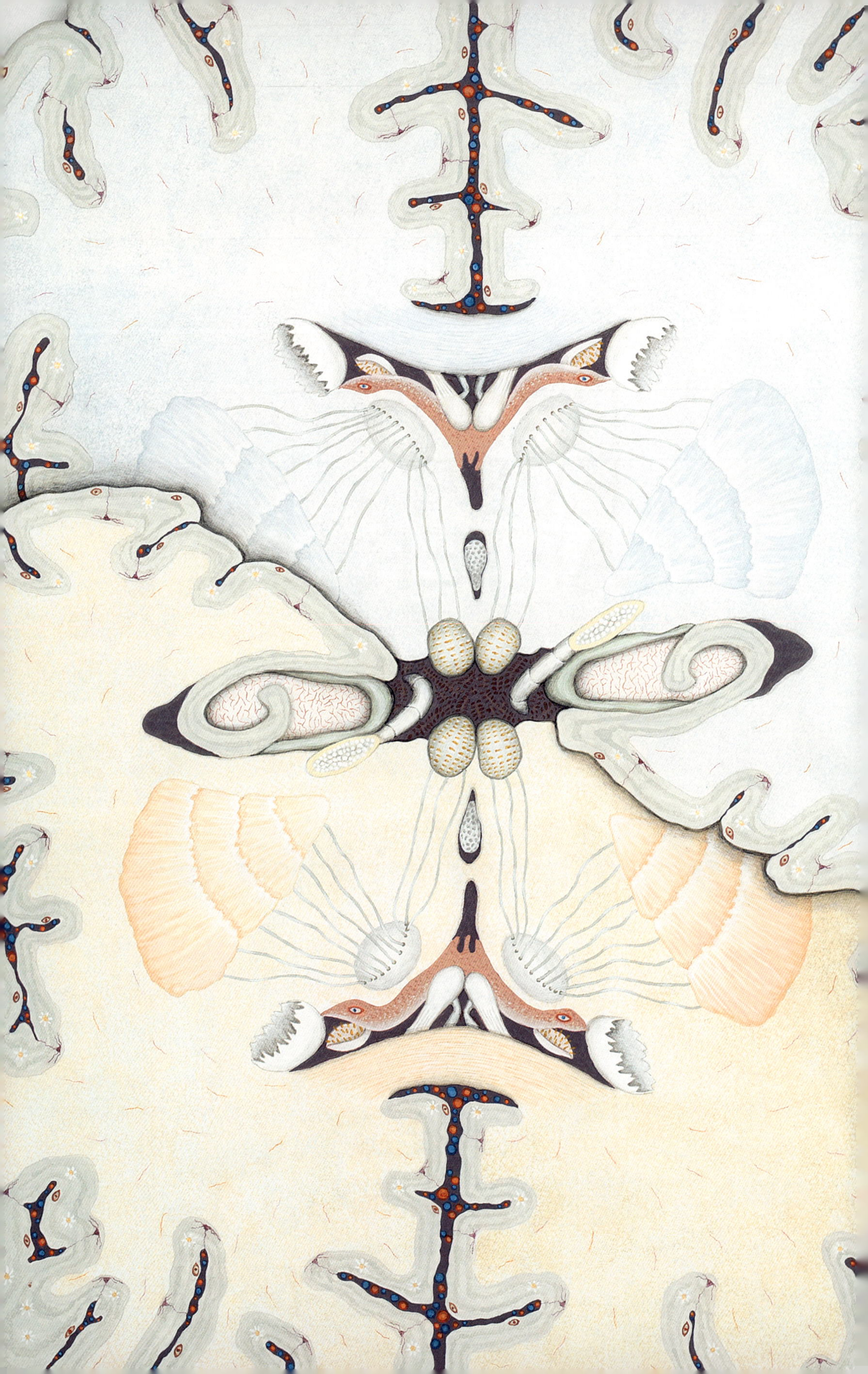

↘Artists:
Muhammad Ali, Anita Christofferssonn, Markus Copper, Jeanne Dunning, Stina Ebers, Elis Eriksson, Helena Fernández-Cavada, Ester Fleckner, Jenny Gronvall, Ramon Guillén-Balmes, Sive Hamilton Helle, Leif Holmstrand, Adelita Husni-Bey, E.B. Itso, Jesper Just, Joachim Koester, Jukka Korkeila, Ellinor Lager, Gloria Lopez Cleries, Truls Melin, Britt-Ingrid Persson BIP, Iris Smeds, Superflex, Hannah Toticki, Ulla Wiggen

Curators: Julia Björnberg & Anna Johansson

Page 3: Jukka Korkeila · Melancholy of a Young Man (detail) · 1996 · Acrylic and charcoal on canvas
Page 4: Ulla Wiggen · Golem III (detail) · 2017 · Acrylic and gold leaf on panel
Page 9: Gloria López Cleries · [ASMR] Reading You to Sleep. Soft-Spoken Relaxation about Affective Capitalism · 2020 · Video still

Contents:

Foreword:

Essays:

Artists & Works:

Foreword

KIRSE JUNGE-STEVNSBORG
Director, Malmö Konstmuseum

The exhibition *Happily Ever After* focuses on how our emotional lives, dreams, and ideals have fallen prey to a multitude of social actors. These actors explicitly, but also implicitly, mobilize emotions in the race to capture our attention. Politicians score points in debates and create allies and opponents with the aid of emotions; companies get us to buy goods and services by alluding to how much better our lives would be with the particular thing they offer. The list can be made long with how everything from working life to social media, dating apps and self-help literature, make us consume emotions and, additionally, be emotionally consumed. Even our values, our world view, and our surroundings are affected by and can be manipulated through emotions. The exhibition addresses the consequences this phenomenon has for us as individuals and as a society. How is the already complex relationship to the self affected by the corruption of our consciousness and our emotions? How do we navigate and resist?

Happily Ever After is an extensive group exhibition with 25 artists and groups of artists who adopt both existential and socially critical perspectives through a range of artistic forms. The exhibition is also a node for conversations and performances that highlight our need to reflect upon ideals, community, empathy, resistance, and vulnerability. This book can be regarded as an extension of the exhibition space and contains presentations of the participating artists. Here, curators Julia Björnberg and Anna Johansson also deepen their reflections surrounding the exhibition. In addition, author and literary scholar Nina Björk contributes with the newly authored essay 'How Optimized Are You?' containing insightful and critical perspectives on the connections between capitalism and emotion.

Malmö Konstmuseum's ambition is to continuously provide new perspectives on its collection and to bring to the fore artworks, artistic practices, and themes in order to be able to reflect upon and analyze critical contemporary questions and problems. Our mission always includes maintaining, exhibiting, and activating the collection, which to date consists of approximately 40 000 works. The exhibition *Happily Ever After* is primarily based upon the collection's contemporary component, with pieces from the 1980s to the present. Through its most urgent theme, the exhibition illustrates the relevance of the collection, how it can be mobilized for a broad audience and, not least, art's ability to provide perspective and create counter-images.

On behalf of Malmö Konstmuseum, I would like to express my warm thanks to the artists Muhammad Ali, Anita Christoffersson, Markus Copper, Jeanne Dunning, Stina Ebers, Elis Eriksson, Helena Fernández-Cavada, Ester Fleckner, Jenny Grönvall, Ramón Guillén-Balmes, Sive Hamilton Helle, Leif Holmstrand, Adelita Husni-Bey, E.B. Itso, Jesper Just, Joachim Koester, Jukka Korkeila, Ellinor Lager, Gloria López Cleries, Truls Melin, Britt-Ingrid Persson BIP, Iris Smeds, Superflex, Hannah Toticki, and Ulla Wiggen. I would also like to thank Beckett-Fonden and Grosserer L.F. Foghts Fond for support, and the museum staff who in a variety of ways have contributed to the production of the exhibition. Last, but not least, thank you to the author Nina Björk, the designers Andréason & Leibel, the translator Jennifer Hayashida, and to the exhibition's curators Julia Björnberg and Anna Johansson.

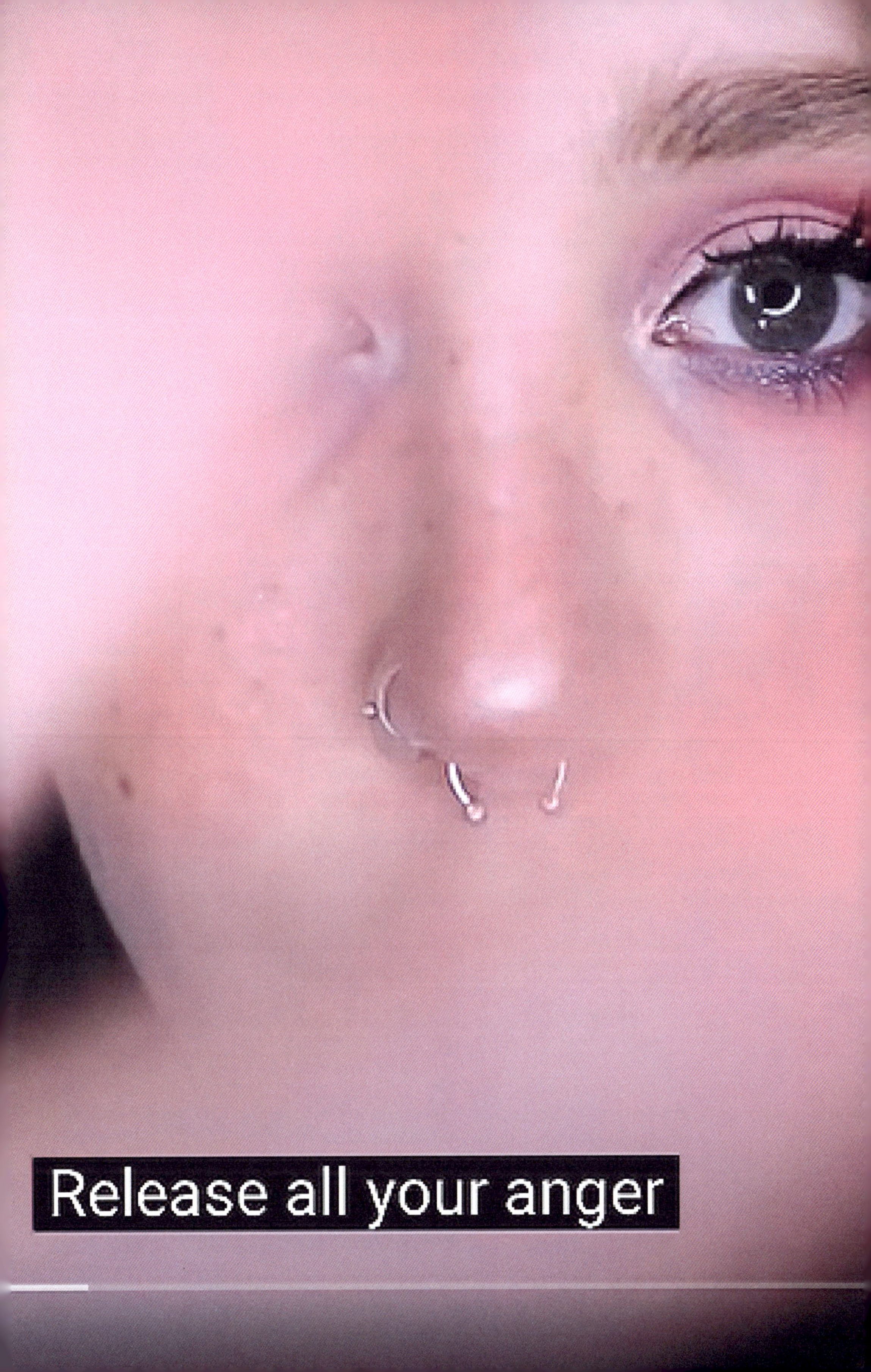
Release all your anger

Happily Ever After—An Introduction

JULIA BJÖRNBERG & ANNA JOHANSSON
Curators

Emotions show us how histories stay alive, even when they are not consciously remembered (...) The time of emotion is not always about the past, and how it sticks. Emotions also open up futures, in the ways they involve different orientations to others.[1]

What happens when our emotions are exploited for profit and control; what are the social consequences and how do we resist? The exhibition *Happily Ever After* shines a light on how different spheres—private and public, emotional and economic—have been woven together in contemporary society. The exhibition brings together artists whose practices explore what happens to us as individuals and collectives in a time cast in a haze of neoliberal optimization of the self, economic and political stakes in our emotions, and an increasing contempt for weakness.

We move through a paradoxical landscape, where we are seduced by and lose ourselves in the dreams and ideals presented by capitalism, to the point where we believe them to be our own. Emotional capitalism has, according to sociologist Eva Illouz, reshaped how we experience and express emotions, and affects our relationship to ourselves, each other, and society around us.[2] Philosopher Byung-Chul Han suggests that we lose sight of the societal situations that can lead to social change since we are so preoccupied with ourselves.[3] It is a landscape where each and every one of us is responsible for our own happiness, which leads to greater separation between human beings and, therefore, less solidarity. The market has taken aim at new forms of production and the psyche has become yet another arena for exploitation. Here, structural problems are time and again displaced onto the individual, who in turn strives to become, 'a permanently happy subject of performance, a subject as insensitive to pain as it is possible to be.'[4]

'You never said that your attention—your emotions, your brain—is for sale. You never said that. Still, your attention is for sale.' Thus begins literary scholar and author Nina Björk her essay 'How Optimized Are You?' included in this book. We have become experts at seeking affirmation and consuming dopamine highs. Hannah Toticki's work *Touch Screen Protection Rings* (2019), consisting of a pair of rings which physically prevent scrolling, can be seen as a retort to this tendency, since use of the rings would compel us to devote time and attention to physical presence with other people instead of our screens.

In the wake of our accelerating existence, sleep deprivation and depression have become ubiquitous social problems, and alternative forms of online therapy such as ASMR (Autonomous Sensory Meridian Response) have gone viral.[5] The artist Gloria López Cleries has immersed herself in this phenomenon through the video series *[ASMR] Reading You to Sleep. Soft-Spoken Relaxation about Affective Capitalism* (2020), presented in the exhibition and on YouTube. With intimate whispers and rustling that are intended to induce shivers, the ASMR-YouTubers perform the artist's critical texts concerning the emotional capitalism upon which the tech industry and social media are founded.

Has the tech industry colonized our consciousness with its promise of never-ending individual freedom and inexhaustible resources? López Cleries and Sive Hamilton Helle examine this notion in the video work *The Unreal* (2019), a guided meditation in a digital mining landscape. The piece addresses how Silicon Valley's techno-capitalism and Californian New Ageism have been integrated into our language, our imagination, and our desires.

As long as you are productive, at work, you are seen as having human value. Your life becomes comprehensible and therefore saleable. For the young athletes in Adelita Husni-Bey's film *After the Finish Line* (2015), life revolves around competition and achievement. To be a top athlete is to be the 'perfect' human being, especially in a US context where the athletic ideal is deeply ingrained in the notion of success. For many, it is also the sole means of gaining access to education. The youth in the film recount what competition means for them and how their self-image has been impacted by injury and failure. Anita Christoffersson's textile work *Mäta—duga* (Measure—Suffice [2015]), processes another type of demand and performance—between mother and daughter and the difficulties of not living up to expectations regarding family and work. The words 'measure' (mäta) and 'suffice' (duga) have been embroidered over and over again across the inherited linen tablecloth. In Iris Smeds' underperforming and nihilistic performance *Death Yoga* (2015/24), death is regarded as the ultimate act of resistance, when we are no longer inclined to produce and perform. Elis Eriksson's painting *Va det allt* (Is That It [2004]), depicts the final stage of life in an elder care facility, where human worth has been replaced by private care companies' pursuit of profit. Everything should be possible to measure and quantify, from cold cuts to diapers and how much time the caregiver can devote to the one being cared for. 'We who are dying are a resource' is the crass statement inscribed upon the painting.

ecome
seeking
mation
suming
e highs

Other points of entry into how emotions are exploited for profit and control are addressed in works by Joachim Koester and E.B. Itso. Koester's two photographs *Untitled (Cocaine #8)* and *Untitled (Cannabis #4)* (both 2019) focus on how narcotics have historically been deployed to control slaves' productivity and hunger, but also how they alter our consciousness and our emotions. An institutionalized form of emotional control is taken to its extreme in E.B. Itso's video installation *The Blue Room (Snake River Correctional Institution)* (2017), which consists of a replica of a cell in an Oregon prison. The cell constitutes one component of a research project exploring if images of nature can make those incarcerated in solitary confinement more harmonious and less violent. The piece illustrates the paradoxical reality the incarcerated are confronted with, since there is evidence that isolation in and of itself is a form of psychological torture which increases violent tendencies in the individual.

In *The Soul at Work* (2009), activist and theorist Franco 'Bifo' Berardi makes the point that workers' feelings of estrangement in the face of labor, their sense of alienation and refusal to comply, previously constituted the basis for a sense of human community which was autonomous in relation to capital. Today, this community and its preconditions have been undermined and a new form of alienation has taken hold, whereby workers often and willingly work overtime, where people are chained to their cell phones, and where indebtedness has become a modern form of slavery.[6] However, in E.B. Itso's photo series *We Resist Therefore We Exist* (2015–21), we see how community can be formed through resistance. The photographs

promise of never-ending individual freedom and inexhaustible resources depict how squatters physically barricade themselves against surrounding society. Alternative communities are also addressed in Ester Fleckner's woodcut series *I Navigate in Collisions* (2014–15). Here, a sense of belonging beyond heteronormative and middle-class norms is mapped through new patterns of social relations.

But how can we actually be ourselves in the production- and perfection-driven society we live in? Where are the spaces where we can show vulnerability? Jesper Just's video work *No Man Is an Island II* (2004) approaches questions concerning the limits of norms surrounding masculinity, including what types of emotions and desires are possible to share with others. Here, lonely men at a strip club forge a kind of temporary community as they together sing Roy Orbison's lovesick ballad *Crying*. Lonely men recur in Jukka Korkeila's paintings, which also consider beauty standards. The bodies in *Melancholy of a Young Man* (1996) and *Cross My Heart and Hope to Die* (2010) do not meet the ideals of Antiquity or Instagram; instead, they appear as counter-images where individuals and vulnerability are foregrounded. In a culture that is increasingly streamlined, where schools as well as the workplace presuppose normativity, Truls Melin's and Leif Holmstrand's works also suggest a need for authenticity. Melin's piece *Untitled* (1998) consists of four cabinets reminiscent of individuals with different characteristics, yet painted in the same shade of pale pink. Holmstrand's *Carpet* (1998), a thick shag rug constructed out of PVC tubing, connotes safety and warmth as well as vulnerability and disgust.

lost in our individual pursuit of happiness and perfection

The ambivalent relationship between self and society is explored by multiple artists in the exhibition. In the years leading up to the Arab Spring and the onset of the war in Syria, Muhammad Ali worked on *Fears Fresh* (2009–11), which depicts the creeping fear that something terrible is about to happen. In the series, Ali has brought together newspaper clippings and messages which he felt warned of what was to come, much like animals seek shelter before the storm. The work was a personal way of managing fear in the face of an imminent war and at the same time gives global fear a new face. Another form of more immediate fear is roused through Markus Copper's interactive sculpture *Knivare* (Knifer [2008]), which in a very straight-forward way addresses socio-political issues by activating feelings in the viewer. How can we attempt to understand the suffering and actions of others if we have not ourselves experienced these emotions? In Britt-Ingrid Persson BIP's sculpture *På fruset vatten—slagruta* (On Frozen Water—Dowsing Rod) from the 1980s, we encounter two astronaut-like figures, each holding a dowsing rod in their hand. Here, the dowsing rod becomes a tool in the relentless pursuit of understanding ourselves, our feelings, and the world around us. With Ulla Wiggen's painting *Världsatlas* (World Atlas [2017]), focus instead turns to the brain and its function as a control system for our emotional lives. The painting depicts four sections of the cerebellum, which controls our ability to act in relation to our surroundings.

The relationship between society and the self is further addressed by Jeanne Dunning and Stina Ebers, but here with the body's limits as a starting point. With the video works *Extra Skin (Adding)* and *Extra Skin (Subtracting)* (both 1999), Dunning seeks an answer to the question of where the self actually exists: is it inside the body or in relation to others? Ebers is also interested in skin as a barrier or container for the self and her work *Hudskulptur* (Skin Sculpture [1986]), consisting of a wood ladder with a painted skin collage, addresses existential conditions and vulnerability.

Seduced by and lost in our individual pursuit of happiness and perfection, we become open targets for the market. In *The Promise of Happiness* (2010), feminist writer and scholar Sara Ahmed writes about what happiness does and how it can be associated with certain life choices, but not others. Happiness becomes an object upon which to project our dreams and fantasies.[7] In Jenny Grönvall's installation and performance *becoming ecru* (2023), aesthetics and notions of 'good taste' are mobilized in terms of how they produce desire in relation to class and our need for a sense of community. She points to the impossibility of letting aesthetic objects and lifestyle concepts determine the relationship to one's well-being. Our economic and political ideology is based on us constantly wanting to have more and 'have it better.' The paradox, however, is if we against all odds were to achieve contentment, the market of services and goods offered would disappear. In the video work *In Order to Eat Another Man's Soul* (2013), Iris Smeds' persona articulates how consumption of food, sex, drugs, and love—and, not least, art—is used as a means to fill empty and chronically hungry souls with contents. The crass reality, where humans' desire for happiness appears synonymous with economic prosperity, can also be found in the painting *Euphoria Now / Swedish Kronor* (2017) by Superflex. Its color spectrum is based on Swedish bills and refers to our time's perhaps greatest hallucination: money.

A counterpoint to the needs the market has created is, for example, Ramón Guillén-Balmes' work *Models for Klaus and Micha* (1997), a series of tools made for people in his surroundings who had expressed a need for or lack of something. The artist regarded these tools as prostheses, operating as extensions of the body and soul. Ellinor Lager's *White Ink No. 23* (2019), which consists of glazed earthenware signs, expresses another need—to liberate oneself from patriarchal language through the representation of one's own physical experiences and memories. Furthermore, Helena Fernández-Cavada's *Looking for a State of Harmony, Although There Is Tension to Be Released* (2022–23) explores how an aesthetic experience can respond to the need for introspection and existential well-being. The series of drawings aims to embody a state of absolute harmony and harbors an inherent hope that it can contaminate its surroundings.

Emotions make us move across the surface of the world and create ripples in the intimate contours of our lives, in the words of Sara Ahmed.[8] They are primary indicators that something is important to us. But how do we know what is important, and how do we navigate, when private and public, emotional, and economic spheres have been woven together? The artworks in *Happily Ever After* operate like a prism in constant movement that affords new points of entry and perspective. The exhibition invites reflection on how emotions can open up futures by emphasizing the importance of resistance in the form of authenticity and community, and how we choose to act in relation to each other.

1 Sara Ahmed, *The Cultural Politics of Emotion*, Edinburgh: Edinburgh University Press, 2004, p. 202.

2 Eva Illouz, *Cold Intimacies: The Making of Emotional Capitalism*, Cambridge: Polity Press, 2007.

3 Byung-Chul Han, *The Palliative Society: Pain Today*, translated by Daniel Steuer, Cambridge: Polity Press, 2021, pp. 10–11.

4 Ibid.

5 The global health organization WHO classifies depression as the third most important cause of poor health in the entire world, and currently estimates that approximately 350 million people suffer from the disease.

6 Franco 'Bifo' Berardi, *The Soul at Work: From Alienation to Autonomy*, translated by Francesca Cadel & Giuseppina Mecchia, Los Angeles: Semiotext(e), 2009, p. 139.

7 Sara Ahmed, *The Promise of Happiness*, Durham: Duke University Press, 2010, p. 2.

8 Ahmed, *The Cultural Politics of Emotion*, p. 202.

How Optimized Are You?

NINA BJÖRK
PhD and author

You never said that your attention—your emotions, your brain—is for sale. You never said that. Still, your attention is for sale.

During large parts of your waking hours, there is someone trying to get into your brain. Wherever you go, wherever you stand, you encounter brand names, advertisements, PR, sponsored posts on social media. What do they want with you? They want your attention. They want your gaze, your interest. For this can be transformed into the most important value of our time and our place: the monetary. Those who buy and sell human attention hunt you and it is difficult to escape—their hunting grounds are our everyday existence, our lives.

When you go to bed at night, what share of everything that has entered your brain during the day have you actively chosen on your own? Maybe you have chosen to read the newspaper or ride public transportation, or listen to a podcast, or look at Instagram and X (formerly known as Twitter). Maybe you have chosen to move around town, maybe to keep your eyes open—but you have not consciously made an effort to find out everything you have found out about. Everything that can be purchased, everything you should desire, all the dreams you ought to make your own. You have been invaded. Your brain has been invaded. Let me out!

Here is how the recipient of the 1974 Nobel Prize in literature, Swedish author Harry Martinson, writes in his novel from 1963, *Views from a Tuft of Grass*, about a child playing with a leaf: 'If you played with a dry leaf, it was meaningful just for what it was—a dry leaf with a great many wonderful qualities. If a wind came up along the ground it could rustle softly, and if you held it up into the air and let it fall, it descended slowly swinging back and forth until it finally reached the grass. It did this only to reveal another fine quality, namely, its lightness and sensitive readiness to move and sway whenever there was the slightest breeze. The whole time it remained within the limits of what a dry leaf is capable of, and just because the child at play remained flexible in his imagination and eyes—and did not require any tremendously remarkable reasons from the leaf—the dry leaf became almost a universal. Thus the leaf could for several minutes, which as a result of the intensity of the experience was transformed into several centuries, fill the child's existence with all the meaning that was required at that moment.'[1]

What is happening here? It happens that a leaf's movements enter a child's mind. Not because the leaf wanted it: the leaf had no intention; it did not try to lure the child. It was the child's consciousness which reached for the leaf and made it large. The child chose the leaf. And so the story ends.

Those of us who are not children during the first half of the 1900s, but adults during the 2020s, seldom choose what enters our heads. Perhaps we choose to look at a screen, but there, we are served anything and everything. There, others have chosen what we should see, and there, others have had objectives for what we should do with what we see. Rarely do we feel free to reach toward something that fills all of existence with intense meaning. We can naturally do what we wish with what we see, but there is most often an idea behind it. Modern technology rarely leaves us as free as that child with the leaf.

And sometimes we truly feel hunted. Then Apple replies, in one of their advertising slogans,

thei

'There's an app for that.' And yes, there is an app for it! For everything! You can purchase courses in mindfulness, pay for a retreat in some gorgeous location; you can purchase noise-cancelling headphones. In North American big cities, where metropolitan electricity brightens the sky to the point that stars are no longer visible, you can go on a 'dark nights tour'—purchase a trip to the countryside to see the night sky.

Growth, acceleration, and innovation—the holy trinity of capitalist society. More, faster, and new. The flight of a leaf through air can hardly contribute anything to that. If a single nation-state does not accept this trinity, it becomes a loser on the global market. If the economy doesn't grow—if we do not produce enough quickly enough, if we do not renew technology and machines—employment opportunities will be lost, companies will go bankrupt, and tax revenues decrease, while state expenditures in the form of subsidies will increase. Then the state budget suffers and the welfare state is threatened. In this economic system, our political freedom of choice is somewhat limited, to put it mildly.

g grounds
everyday
existence

Do people always enjoy doing more things faster? Do people always want to have the latest, do and embody the latest? No, not necessarily. Can people still be made to strive for it? Yes.

Not because some king, prime minister, or priest preaches to you. No one says: growth, acceleration, and innovation are the goals you must realize in your life. No one says that you are personally responsible for increasing our nation's BNP. There are no stone tablets where such laws are inscribed. When we still obey, when we still strive for growth, acceleration, and innovation, it is because the laws of the stone tablets have moved into our hearts. For there, in our hearts, we can feel what humans actually always feel, regardless of the national economy: we feel and want to have worth, belonging, and the appreciation of others. And we receive worth, belonging, and the appreciation of others by striving for particular goals and by being human in particular ways. What these goals are and what kind of subjectivity we are talking about varies according to different historic, economic, and cultural contexts. But all societies have their explicit or unspoken ideals and notions of what constitutes a successful life.

In our particular time and place it is, for the individual, rooted in such things as having an entrepreneurial subjectivity, being a 'project-self,' being flexible, goal-oriented, open to change, and constantly available for the world to reach—to work to optimize oneself and one's actions.

The trinity of growth, acceleration, and innovation together constitute perhaps one of the most important values of our time: efficiency. The problem with efficiency is that humans tend to perform less well in that arena than technology does: we somehow risk falling short in comparison with these amazingly efficient thingamajigs. Machines, robots, computers, and smart phones have no feelings and no history: they are dead—and super-efficient—things. And, to boot, their results are measurable.

n proper numbers, we can see: good perfor-mance or bad performance.

Humans can never become like machines; our fate is not theirs. Nonetheless, we still use them as a kind of ideal: we hold them close and make some of their abilities our own. They help us increase our efficiency, become a bit more machine-like.

We can, for example, measure our performance thanks to them. We can count our steps, our pulse, how many calories we burn, our sleep. And so human spheres, which previously had nothing to do with measurement or achievement or comparison, are drawn into the kingdom of efficiency. We have internalized demands for everything-faster, everything-better: we want them, we desire them. When everything can be measured, everything can be known—and it will always be possible to perform.

Even a night out with friends. Among other things, the American company Fitbit markets a step counter that uploads your movement data. A few years ago, an image on their website showed a group of young people dancing at what appeared to be a club or perhaps an outdoor party at twilight. The caption reads: 'How you spend your day determines when you reach your goals. And seeing your progress helps you see what's possible.' Not even at a party, not even while dancing, are you allowed to forget your goals—which naturally cannot be something like 'being at a party,' but, as Apple reminds us: 'Every move counts. So count every move.' As the media and communications scholar Steffen Krüger reminds us in the article where I found this

Not even at a party, not even while dancing...

example, 'Spheres of play are becoming vetted for their capacity to maintain the individual in the best possible relation to reality. Notions of competition and rational choice, the two main pillars of neoliberalism, are introduced into spheres that have traditionally been seen to offer respite from such preoccupations.'[2]

A dancing body is no longer something you simply *are*—it is something you *have*. Something you own and ought to take care of, manage properly. Just as we ought to manage our sleep, our rest, our emotions. Yes, everything we do now share with those efficient technological gadgets and which therefore can cause trouble in our social—and internalized—striving. We must control such human, all too human, phenomena.

And we try! We struggle! We measure, optimize, meditate, work out, schedule time for recreation and socializing. All according to plan. And in spite—or because of—this, we fall, many fall. More and more anti-depressants are prescribed, more and more sleeping pills, more and more sick leave due to burnout. Human sacrifices upon the altar of efficiency.

It is as if we do not understand—as if we cannot afford to understand—that there are things which cannot be optimized, rationalized, hurried up, and renewed. Care, for example. When one human takes care of another—a little one, or an old or sick human—we cannot measure what transpires between them us ing the metric of 'efficiency.' We can certainly measure how long it takes to change a diaper or serve a meal, but we cannot measure the eye contact between those involved, the conversations, the contact—the relationships. No matter if the caring takes place in the private realm or in the workplace for pay, the metric of 'efficiency' is wrong.

We can understand this idea. We can agree with it. But the risk is that the result of this kind of understanding becomes a devaluation of the sphere of care itself. A sphere that cannot *be* optimized: isn't that hopelessly old-fashioned and outdated? Isn't *everything* that cannot be made more efficient hopelessly old-fashioned and outdated?

Uh-oh, a suspicion rears its head: what if this also pertains to human beings?! What if the only thing worth preserving in a human being is that within her which lets itself be optimized, altered, made efficient? No, we know that this isn't the case. We know that human beings are wide open fields, that we have many facets, many needs. Some of them can be updated and compliantly follow their time—some cannot. We just need to remember that we are in a situation where what we need to defend within us is what cannot be updated and made more efficient. And this is necessary since the model for the human in just our place and just our time appears to be the machine, ever so efficient.

I write the word 'preserve' well aware of the fact that it is adjacent to the word 'conserve'—and therefore also the more politically fraught term, 'conservative.' I do not see myself as politically conservative, do not believe that something existing for a long time necessarily means that it has inherent value. But I also mean that the opposite holds true: the idea that something is novel, of its time, and updated does not automatically mean that this something is of value.

We return to Harry Martinson's child and leaf. There, nothing was new, updated, or profitable—neither the child nor the leaf. But that the child could fix its attention on something as ordinary as a leaf in the air—*that* is worth preserving. To conserve. The attention a human directs at something without someone else, with the goal of turning a profit, having made an effort—*that* is worth preserving. My advice: set your eye on what you yourself have chosen.

...are you allowed to forget your goals

1 Harry Martinson, *Views from a Tuft of Grass*, translated by Lars Nordström & Erland Anderson, Copenhagen & Los Angeles: Green Integer Books, 2005.

2 Steffen Krüger, 'The Authoritarian Dimension in Digital Self-Tracking—Containment, Commodification, Subjugation,' in *Lost in Perfection*, edited by Vera King, Benigna Gerisch & Hartmut Rosa, New York: Routledge, 2019.

Artists & Works:

Stina Ebers

HUDSKULPTUR (SKIN SCULPTURE)
1986 · Wood, lacquer · Acquired 2020

The skin is the human body's largest organ. It protects our bodies against bacteria, viruses, and the sun. Expressions such as 'being thick-skinned' or 'having skin in the game' are based on the notion of skin as protection and as a barrier in terms of emotional stress. Stina Ebers' *Hudskulptur* (Skin Sculpture) consists of a found wooden ladder that has been painted like a collage, or puzzle, of skin flaps, joined to form a covering surface. In the work, which addresses human existential conditions and vulnerability, body and abstraction encounter the symbolism of both the ladder and the skin. In later works, such as *Arbetsdräkt för människan* (Worksuit for the Human [1995]), she continues to work with skin collage, but then through an overall for humans to wear, perhaps as an extra protective layer. Ebers often deploys unconventional materials and combinations, such as a ladder and nail polish, or asphalt, felt, and waste oil.

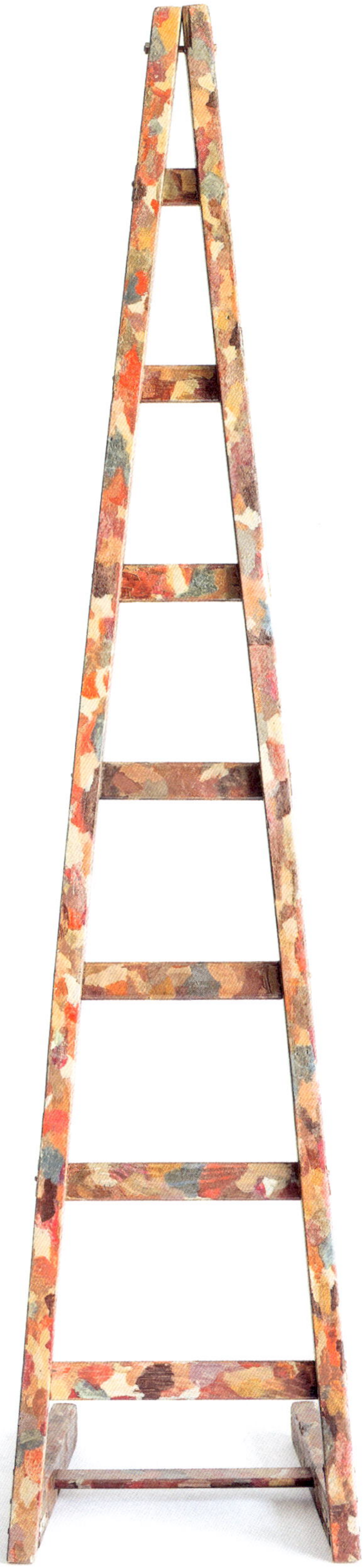

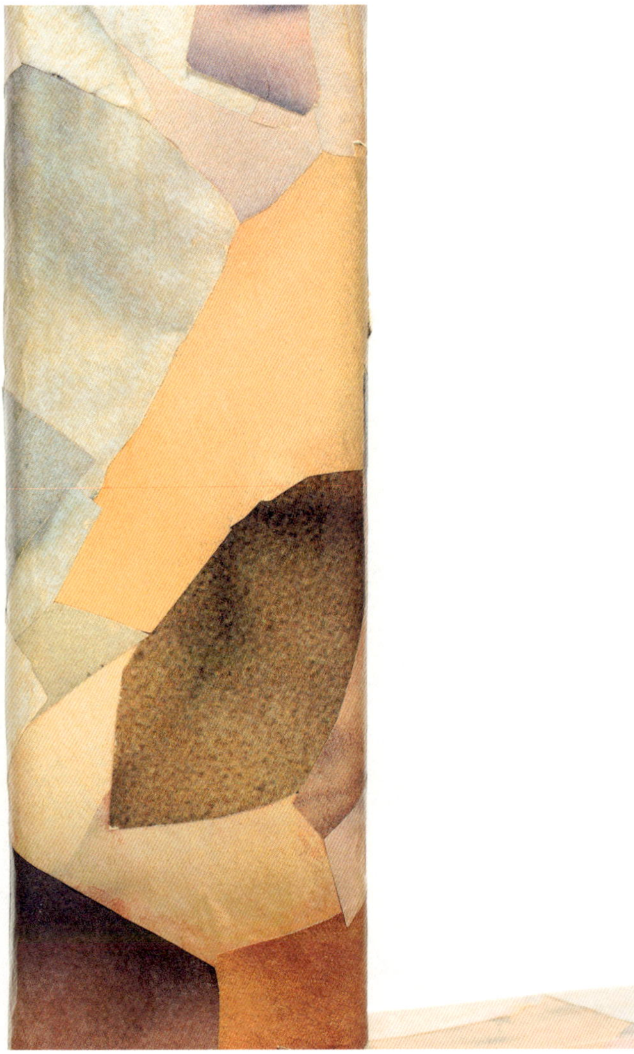

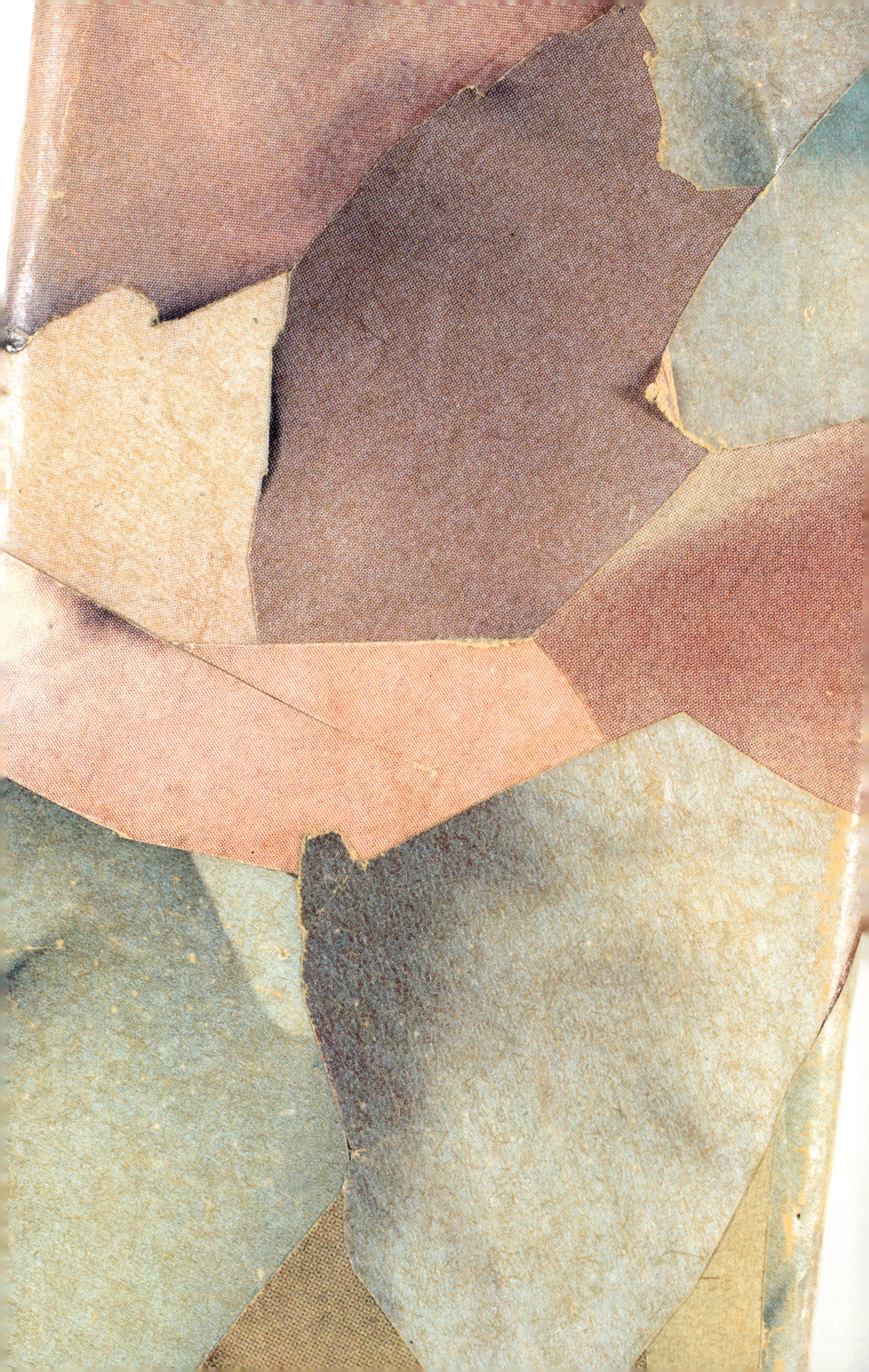

Gloria López Cleries & Sive Hamilton Helle

THE UNREAL
2019 · Machinima film (13:50 min) · Acquired 2023

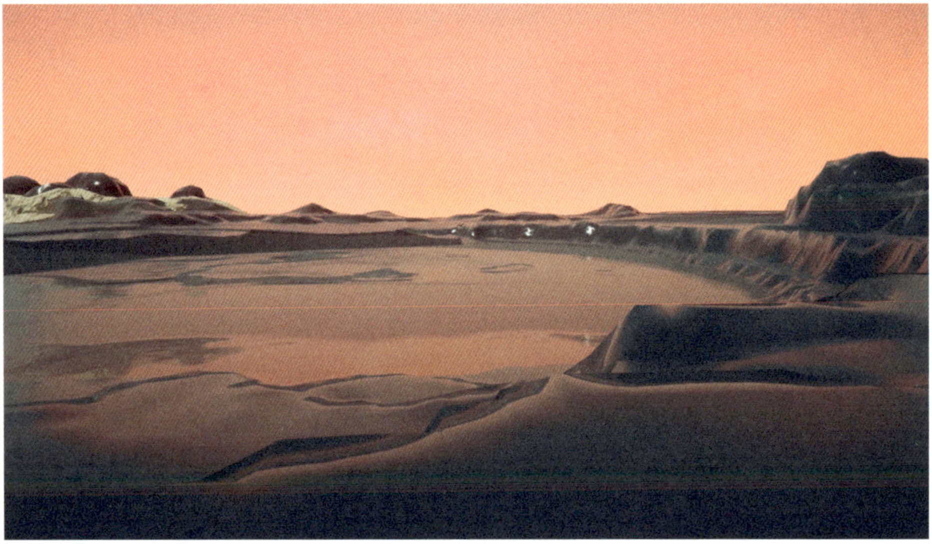

Imagine floating in an infinite and weightless space for your desires and your individual freedom. In the artificial mining landscape of *The Unreal*, a video work where the visuals are created through the game engine Unreal Engine, the sky never ends. In *The Unreal*, a guided tour through a digital landscape is simulated parallel with a guided meditation and ambient music. The work shows how the meeting between Silicon Valley's techno-capitalism and Californian New Age has become integrated into our use of language, our imagination, and our desires. Can we imagine a landscape that is not colonized or exploited, even in fictional spaces? Through this project, Hamilton Helle and López Cleries test the idea that the tech industry has colonized our consciousness with its promise of infinite resources. They also point to how technology both appropriates and impoverishes nature.

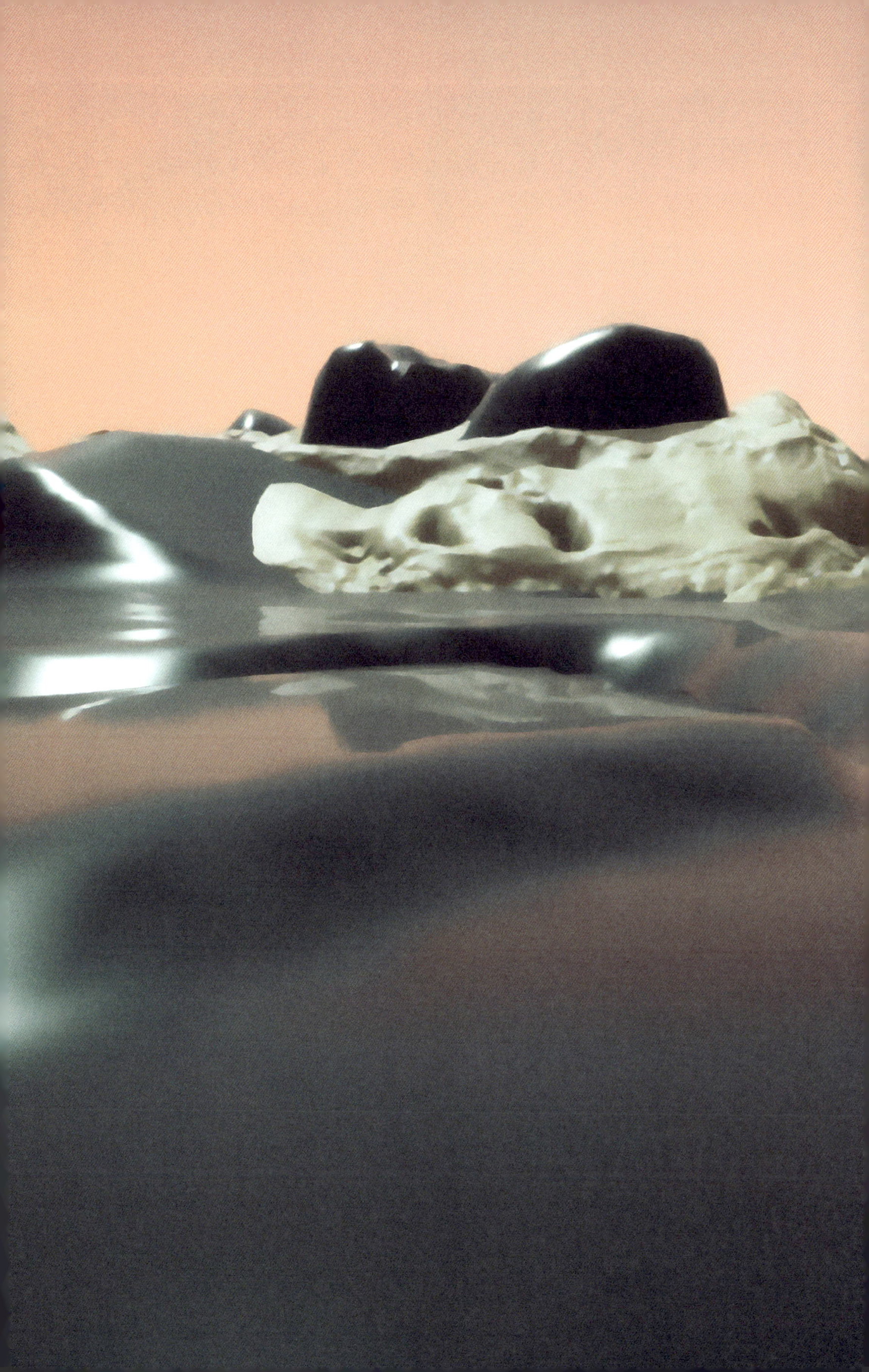

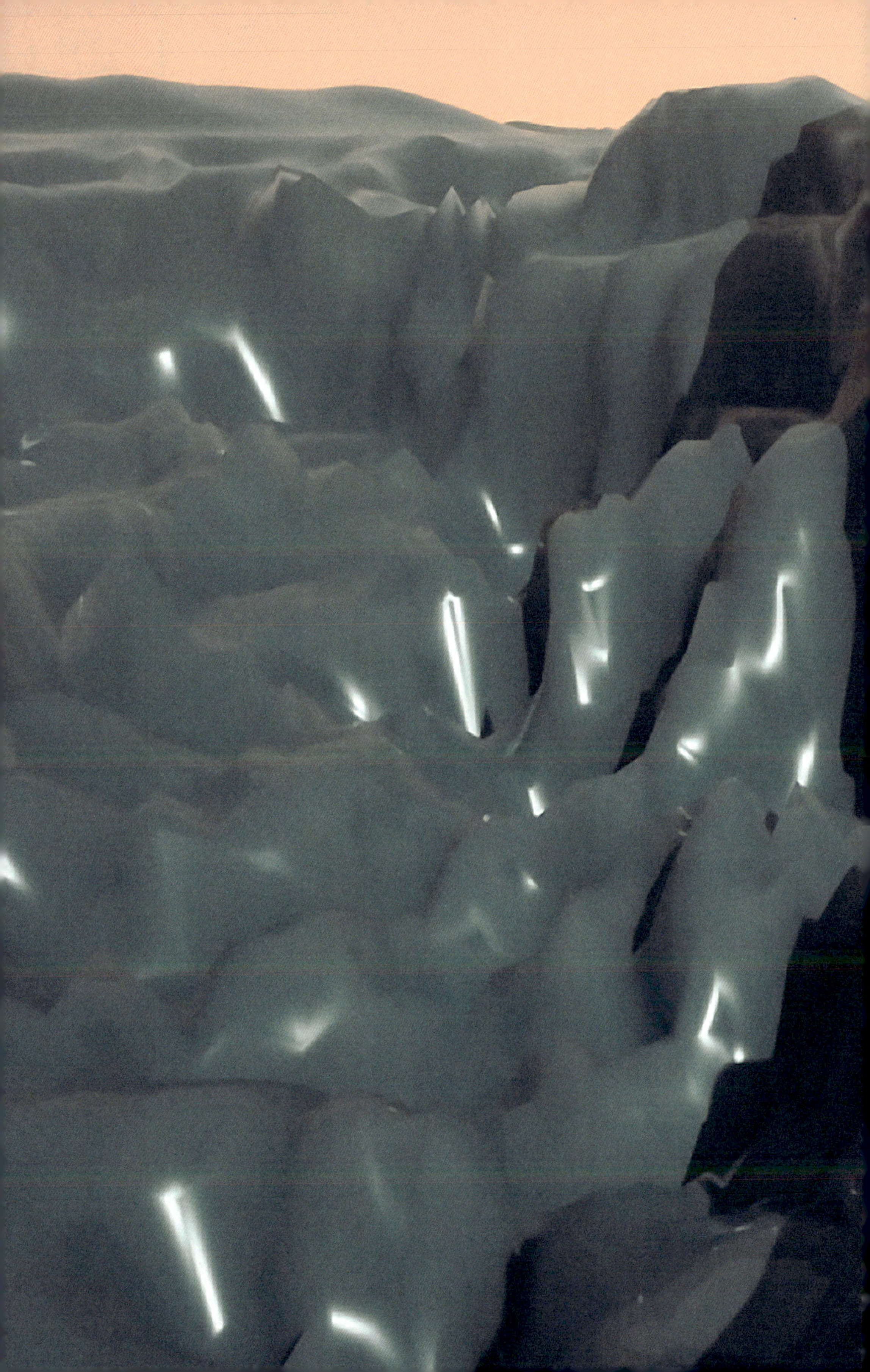

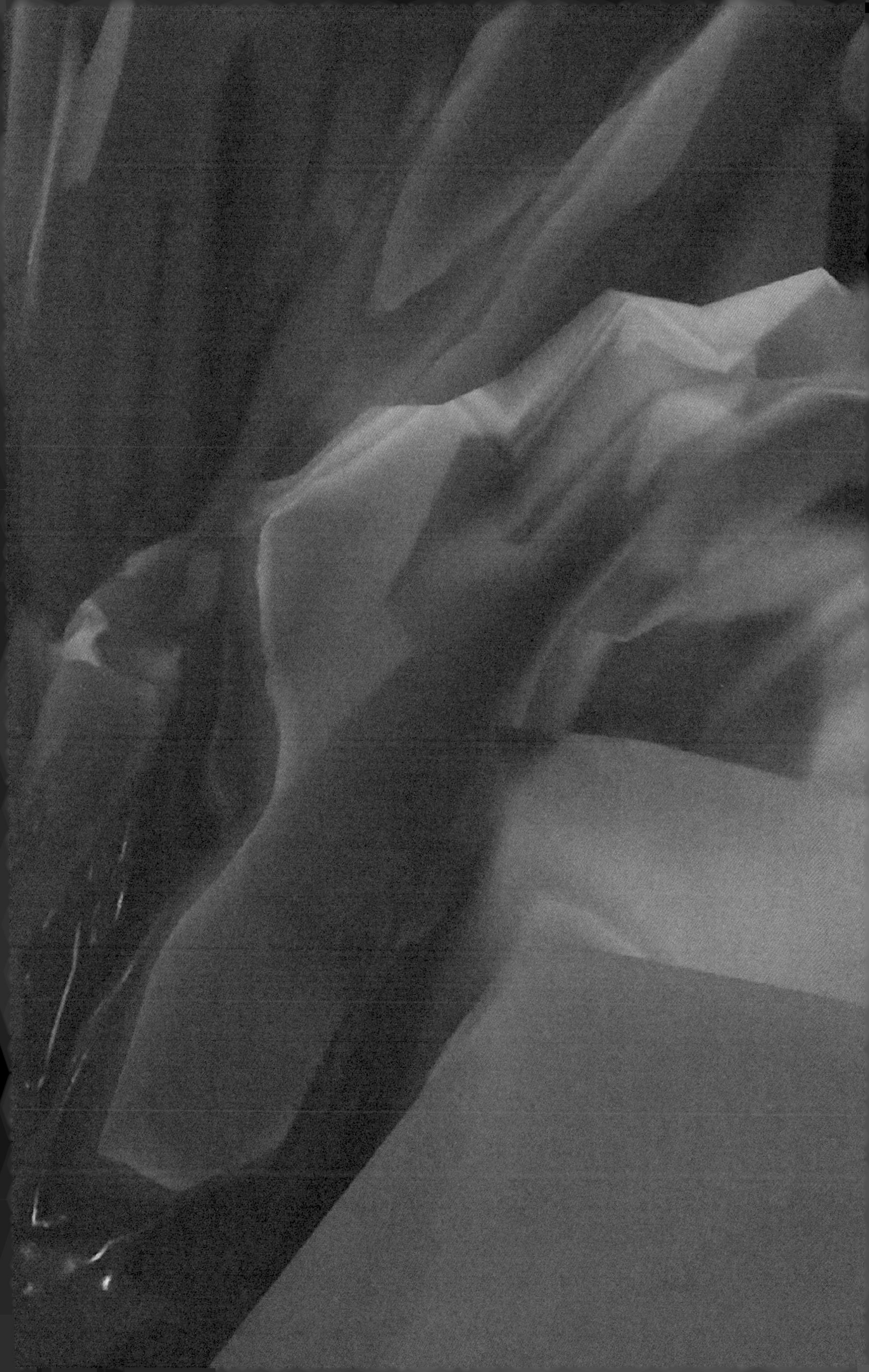

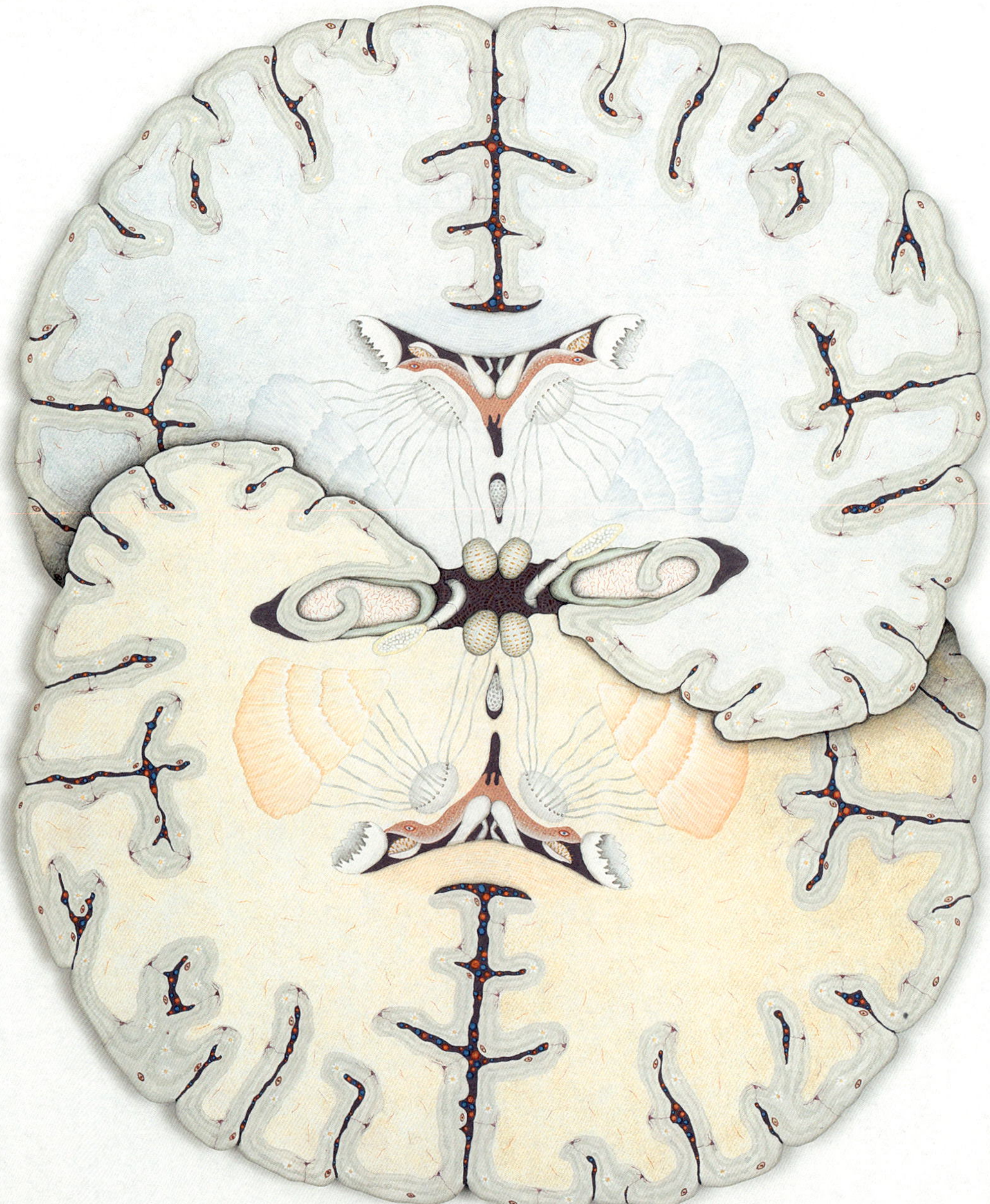

Ulla Wiggen

GOLEM III
2017 · Acrylic and gold leaf on panel · Acquired 2017

VÄRLDSATLAS (WORLD ATLAS)
2017 · Acrylic and gold leaf on panel · Acquired 2018

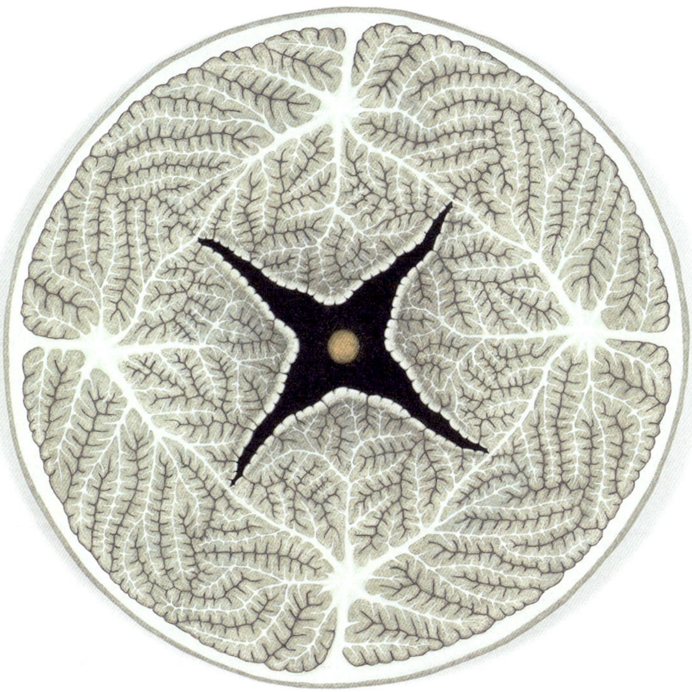

Ever since Ulla Wiggen emerged as an artist in the 1960s, she has devoted herself to painting a range of intricate systems. Early in her career, she became interested in the interior of computers, which she painted with detailed brushstrokes. In recent years, her focus has been on the human interior, such as the eye and the brain. The work *Golem III* (p. 28) consists of two slowly rotating brain hemispheres and invites the viewer to consider the function of the brain as a control system for our emotional lives. The piece also references Jewish folklore, where Golem, an anthropomorphic man-made creature symbolizes an embryo-like unfinished state.

The work *Världsatlas* (World Atlas [pp. 29–31]) consists of four sections of the cerebellum. A black hole opens up around a golden orb at the center of the circle, as a symbol of the unknown we all face. The cerebellum makes up one-tenth of the brain and controls balance and motor skills. Recently, research has also shown that the cerebellum is crucial to our thinking and emotional life.

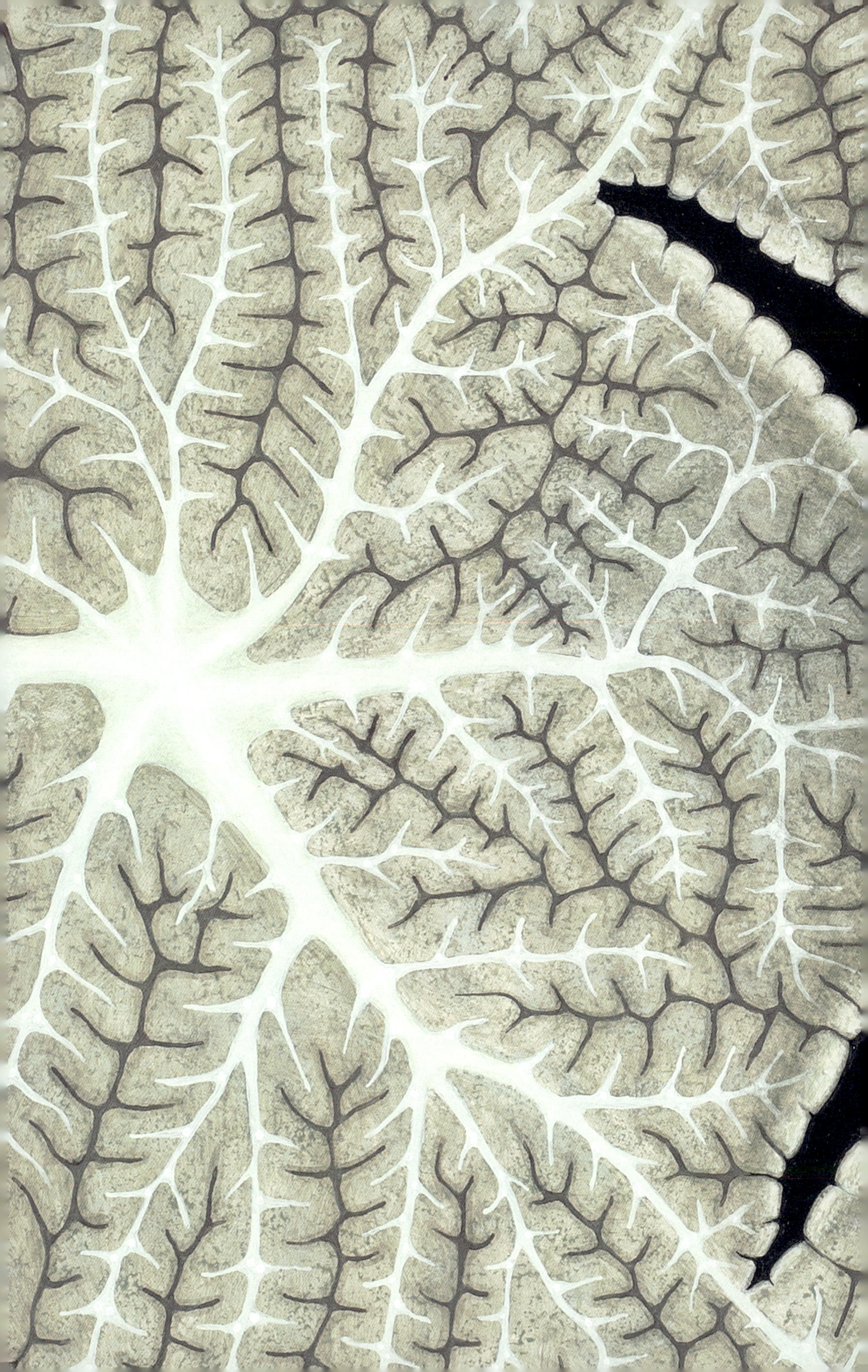

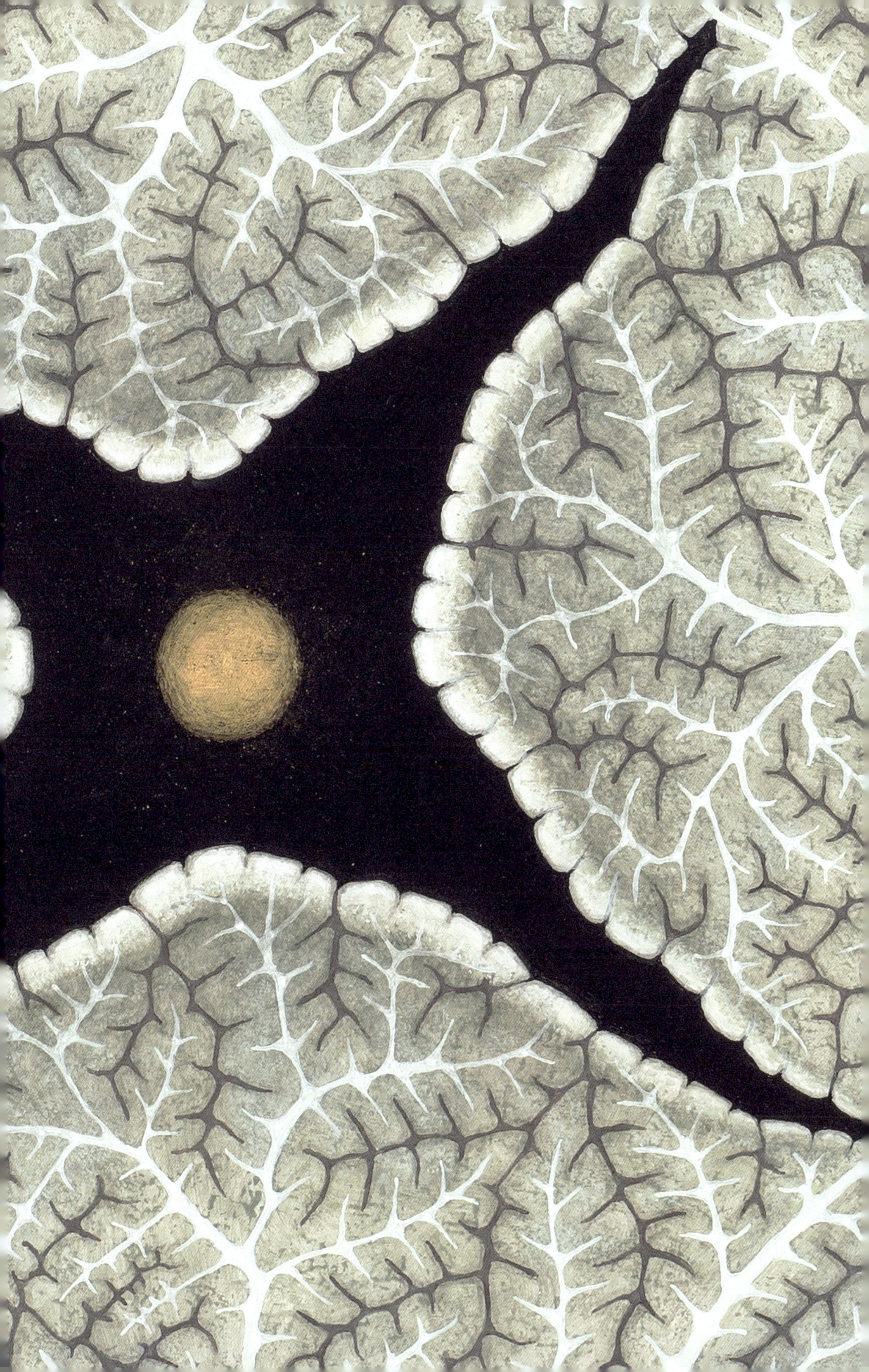

Superflex

EUPHORIA NOW / SWEDISH KRONOR
2017 · Enamel, spray paint and acrylic on canvas · Acquired 2019

Euphoria Now is a series of paintings by Superflex, based on the color spectrum found in the currencies of the global market. In addition to the Swedish version shown in the exhibition, the group has also made works based on the euro, the US dollar, the yuan, and the British pound. In *Euphoria Now* there are also connections to Brion Gysin's and Ian Sommerville's invention Dream Machine (1958/95) which highlighted the hypnotic effects of various patterns that arise when we look at flickering lights, which they believed could encourage artistic production. With the series, Superflex has transformed the concept of the dream machine into perhaps the most hypnotic hallucination of our time—money. The title of the work is written across the painting in the same style as the iconic poster for Francis Ford Coppola's film *Apocalypse Now* (1979), to evoke the euphoric effects sought by the global market as well as the apocalyptic moods that follow in its aftermath.

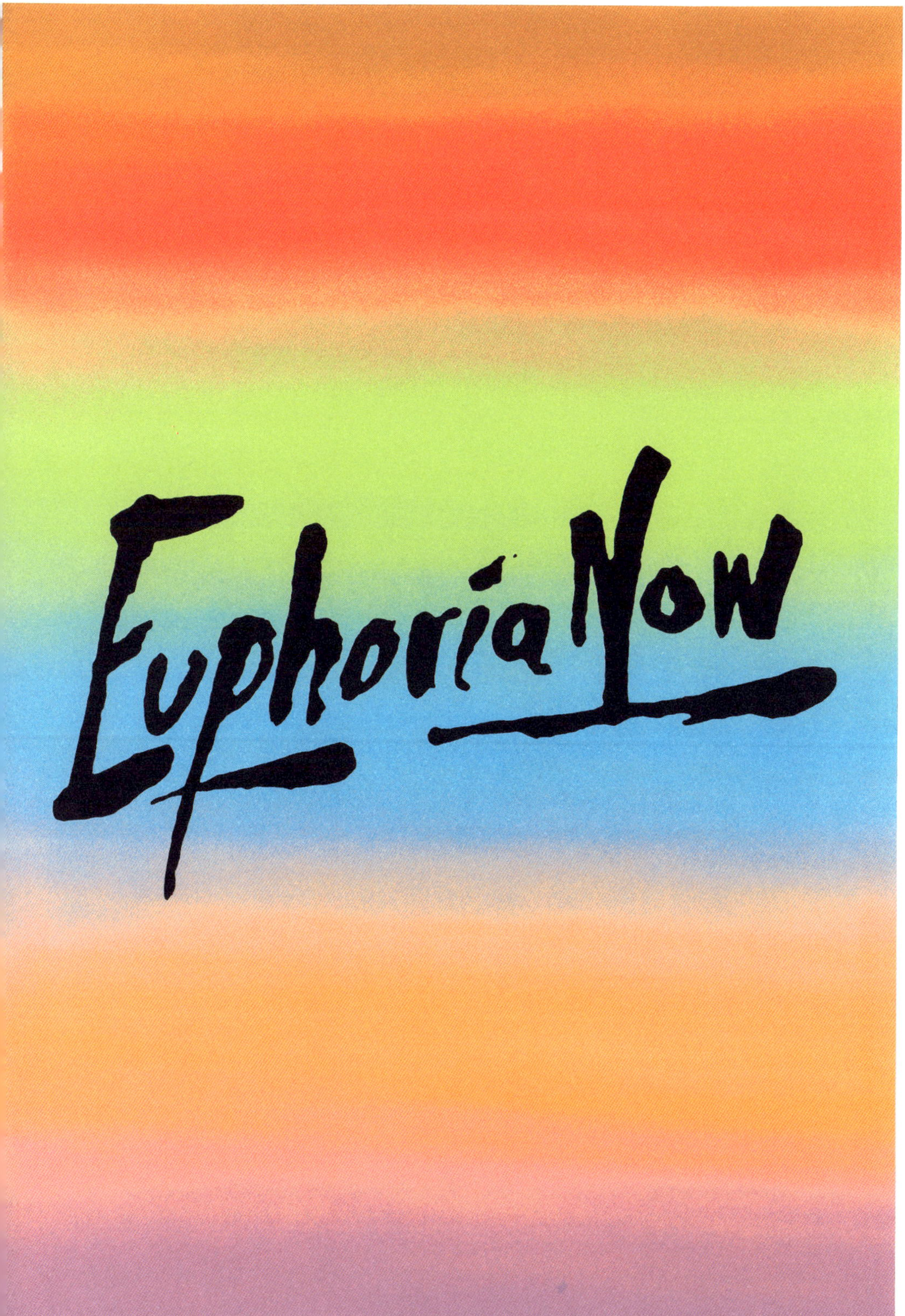
Euphoria Now

Jukka Korkeila

CROSS MY HEART AND HOPE TO DIE
2010 · Oil on canvas · Acquired 2010

SOMEWHERE THERE IS ALWAYS SOMEONE CRYING
1996–97 · Oil and acrylic on MDF · Acquired 1998

MELANCHOLY OF A YOUNG MAN
1996 · Acrylic and charcoal on canvas · Acquired 2000

Jukka Korkeila often works with collisions or hybrids between the private and the public and notions linked to gender and sexuality. Many of his paintings, such as *Somewhere There Is Always Someone Crying* (pp. 36–37, detail), are both abstract and representational, loaded with emotion, fragments, and floating body parts. In a situation where others cannot, for various reasons, cry, it is according to Korkeila the artist's job to do it for them. The function of the weeper was to prepare for mourning and prompt collective weeping in both the ancient and Karelian tradition of weepers.

Melancholy of a Young Man (pp. 38–39, detail) and *Cross My Heart and Hope to Die* (p. 35, detail) both touch upon toxic masculinity and its limiting norms. The men depicted in the paintings do not correspond to the beauty standards that come from the Greco-Roman sculptural tradition or Instagram's physical ideals, but rather become counter-images where individuals and vulnerability are foregrounded.

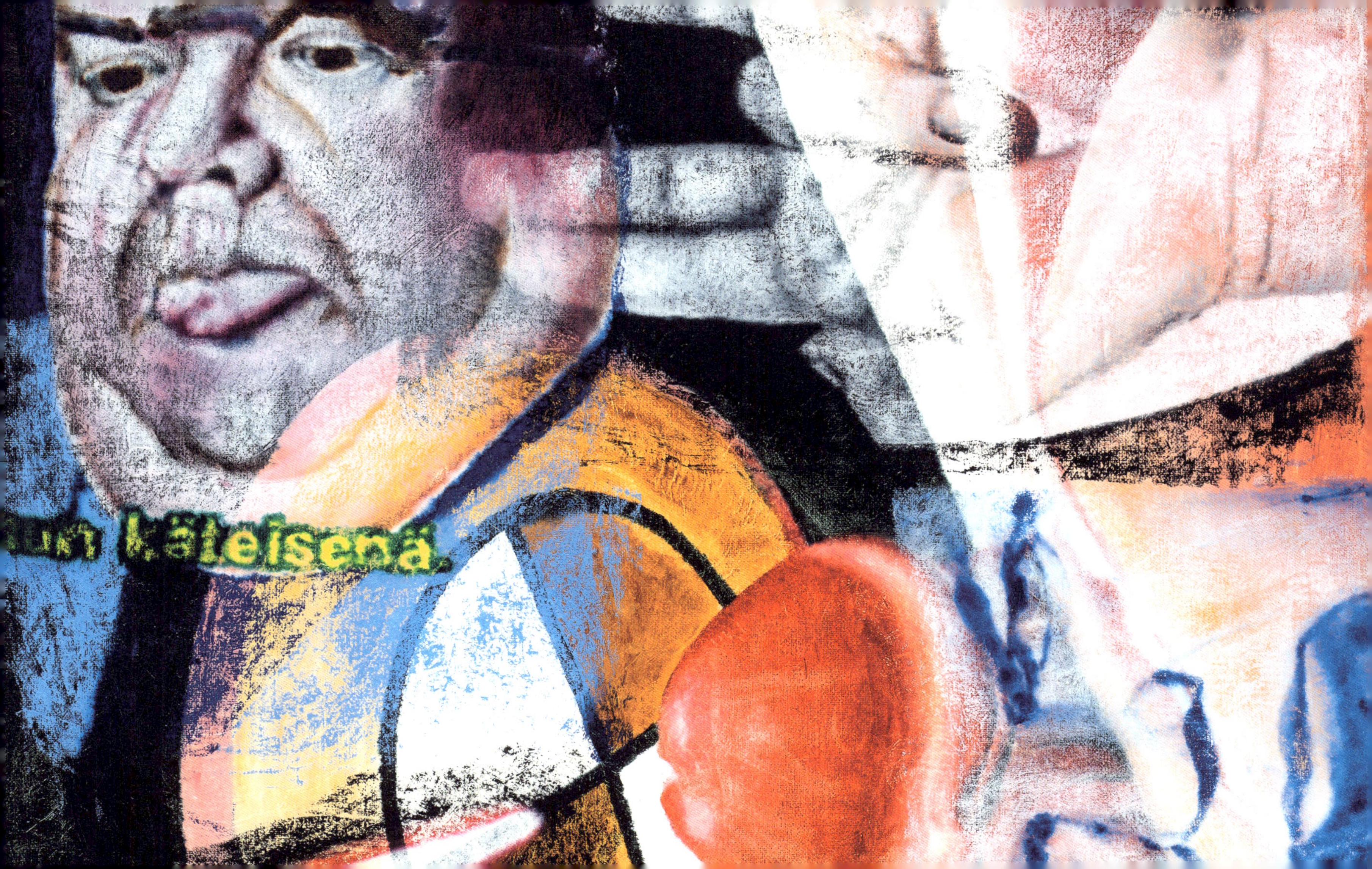
un käteisenä.

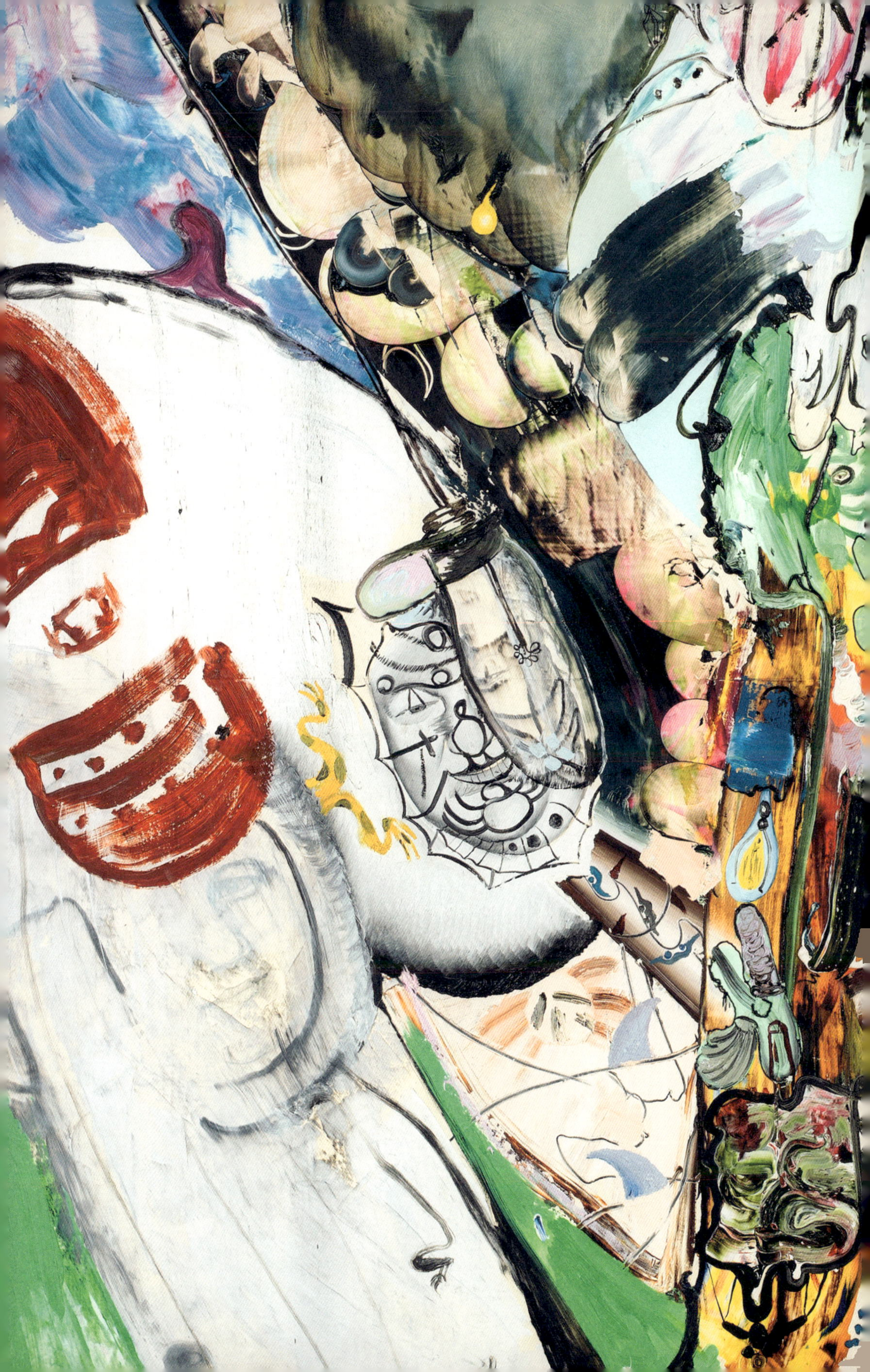

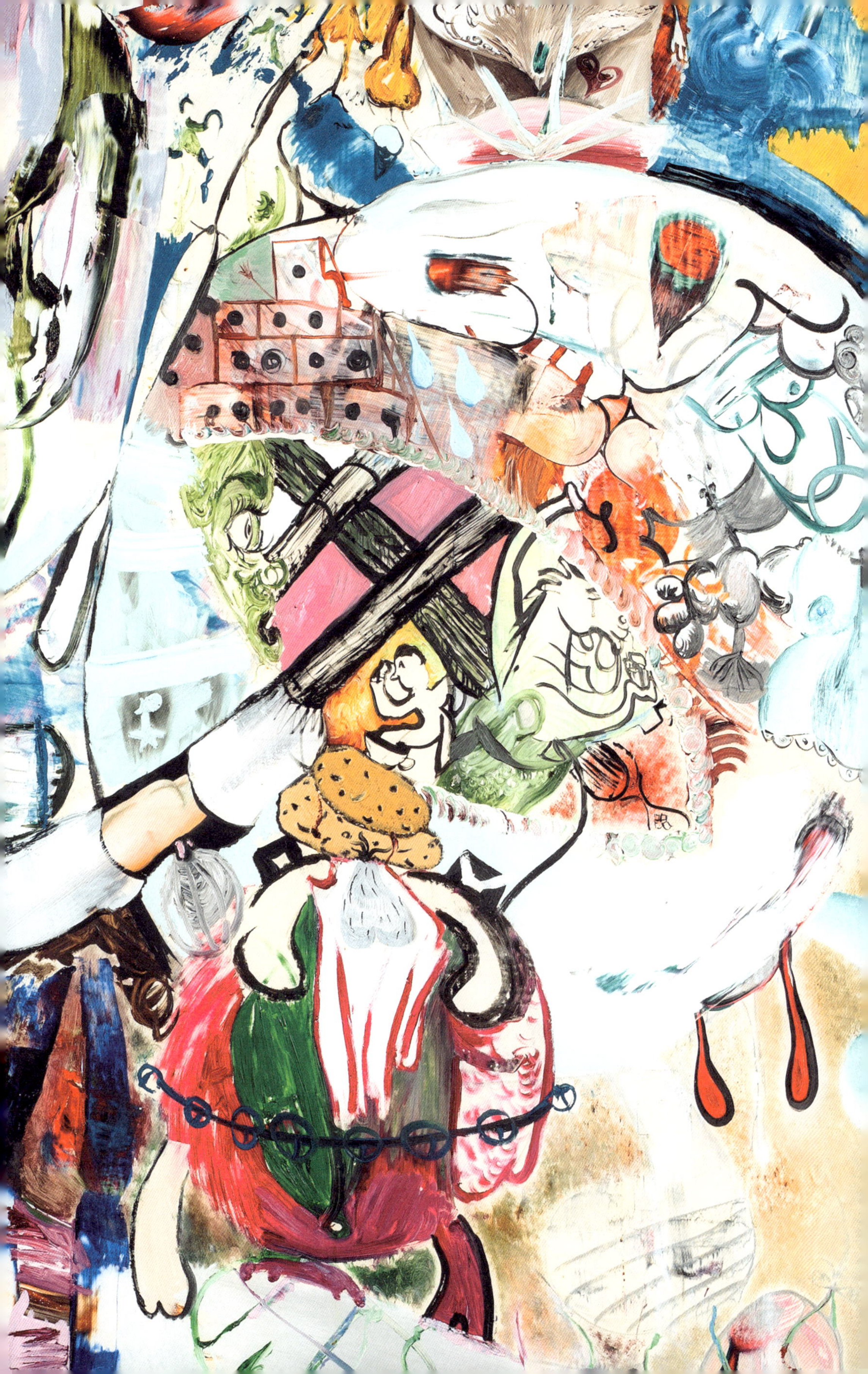

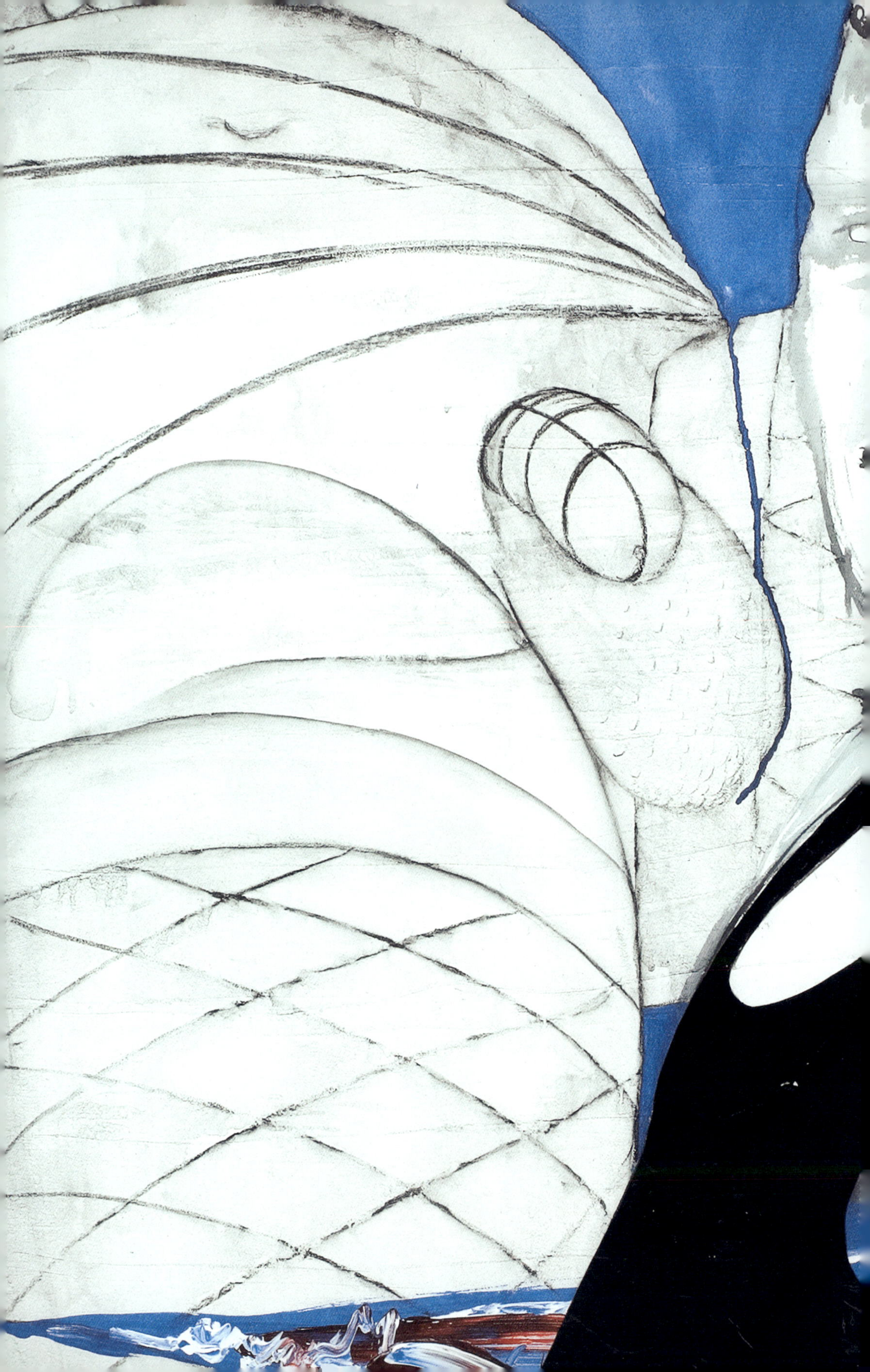

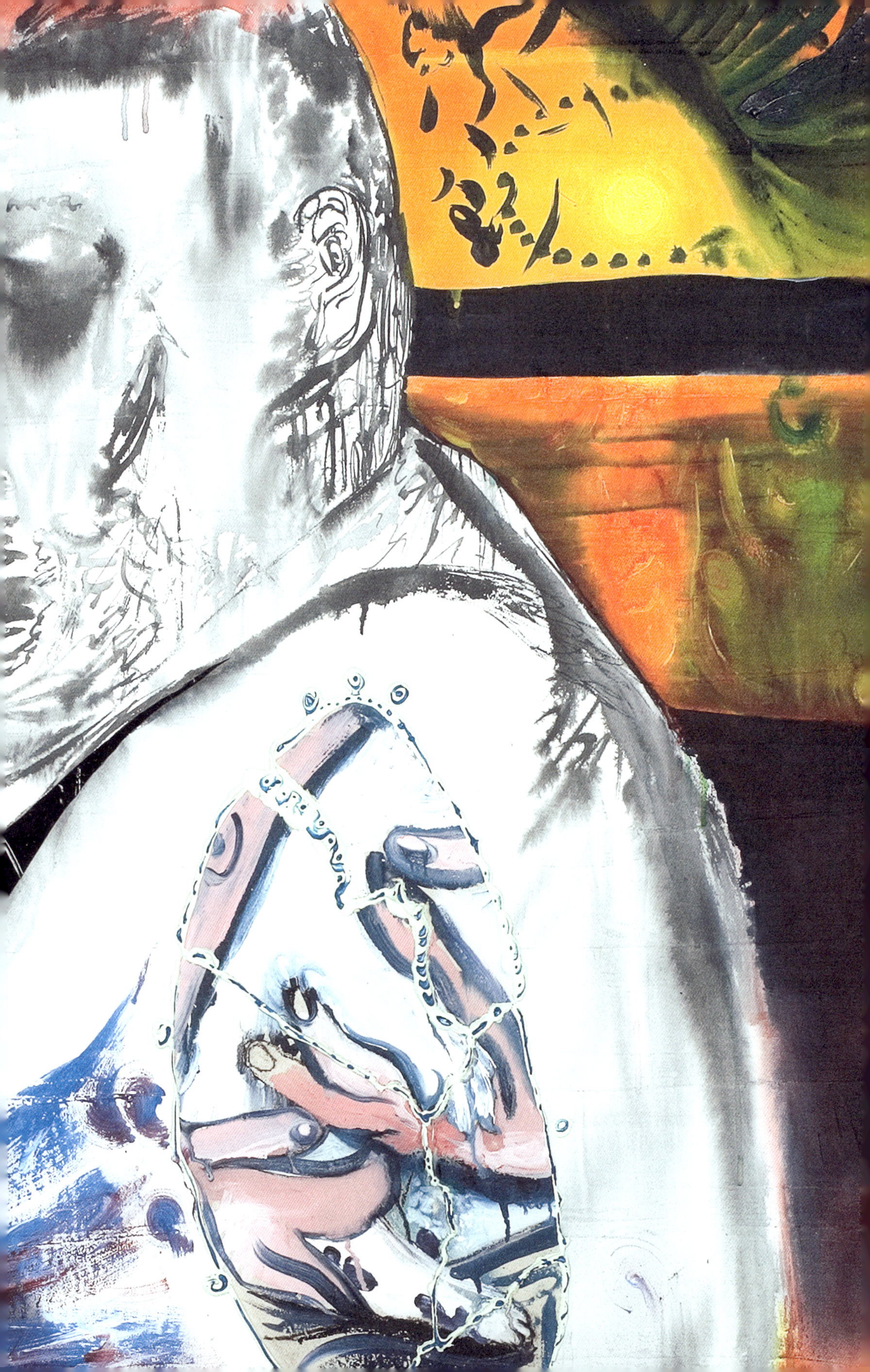

Ester Fleckner

I NAVIGATE IN COLLISIONS
2014–15 · Woodcut on paper · Acquired 2017

The opening work in Ester Fleckner's series *I Navigate in Collisions* consists of a text that touches upon feelings of belonging and the lack thereof. 'I think about pedigree. And about having read that it requires synchronization with a city's patterns and rhythms in order to feel that you belong,' read two lines. Fleckner's practice navigates trans, queer, and crip perspectives through abstraction and a dissolution between written and bodily language. In the earlier work *Clit-dick Register* (2013–14), the artist suggests both new and multiple meanings of existing signs, for example that a U can be read as the letter U, but can also denote genitalia beyond binary divisions. The U reappears, as does the asterisk denoting the anus, in *I Navigate in Collisions*. The series consists of abstract relational patterns that play with the figure of the traditional heterosexual and bourgeois family tree or pedigree. Fleckner comments, 'To navigate in collisions is to navigate outside straight and linear relational patterns, to create new and different connections and ways of belonging.'

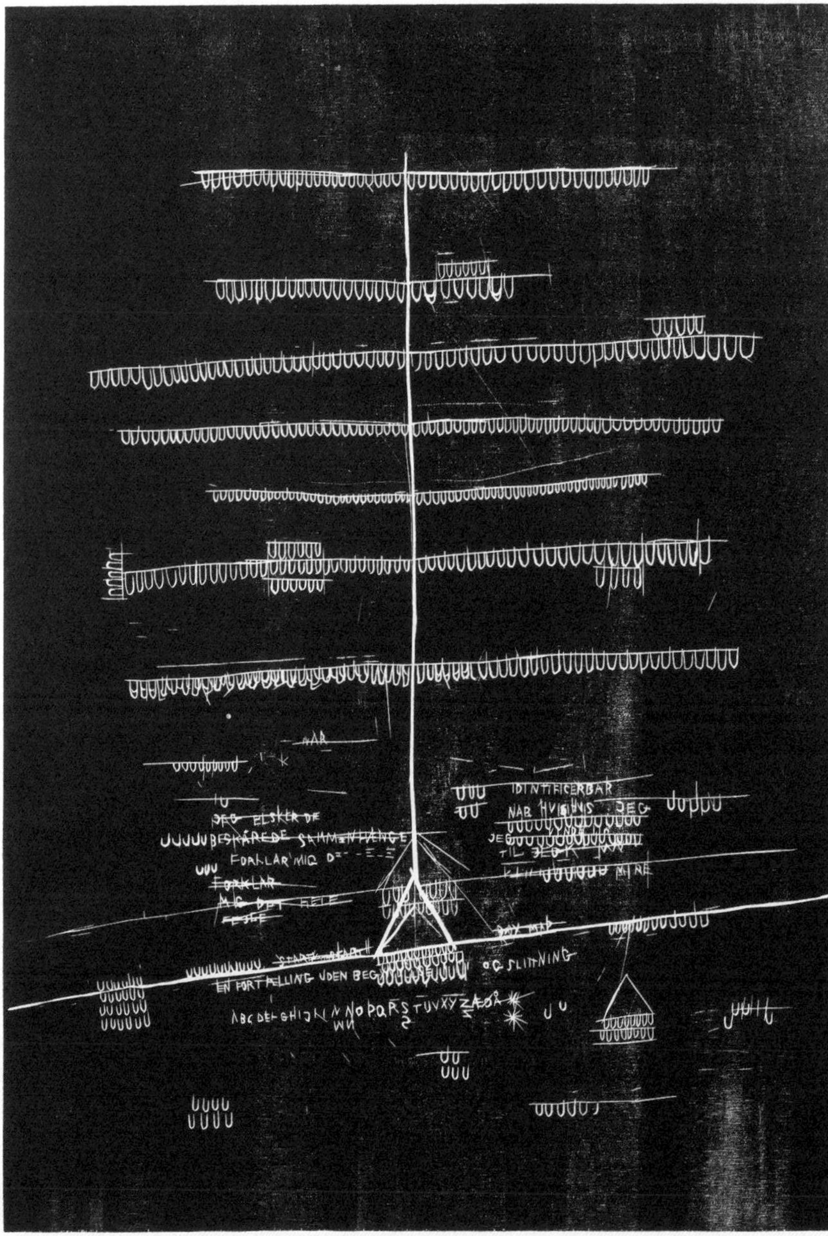
NAR
JEG ELSKER DE
BESKÅREDE SAMMENHÆNGE
FORKLAR MIG
FORKLAR
IDINTIFICERBAR
NAR
JEG
TIL
MINE
OG SLITNING
EN FORTÆLLING UDEN BEG
ABCDEFGHIJ NOPQRSTUVXYZÆØÅ

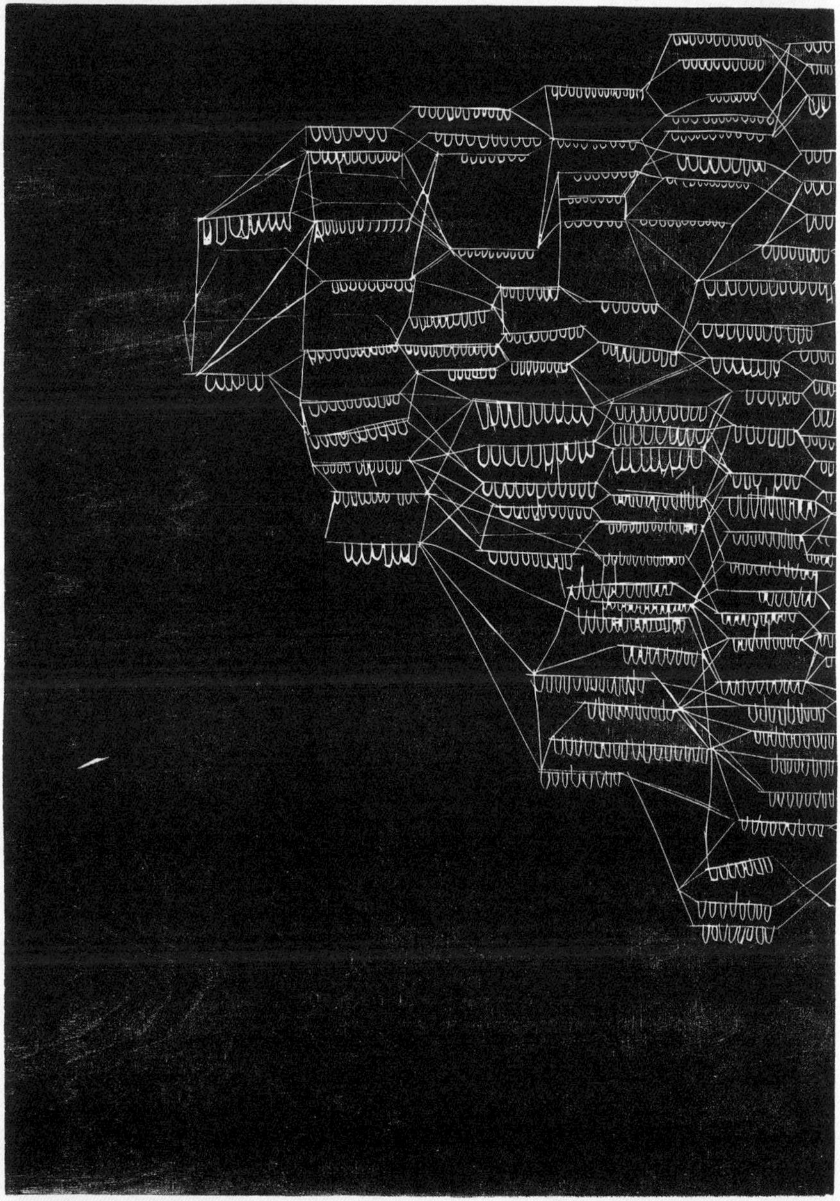

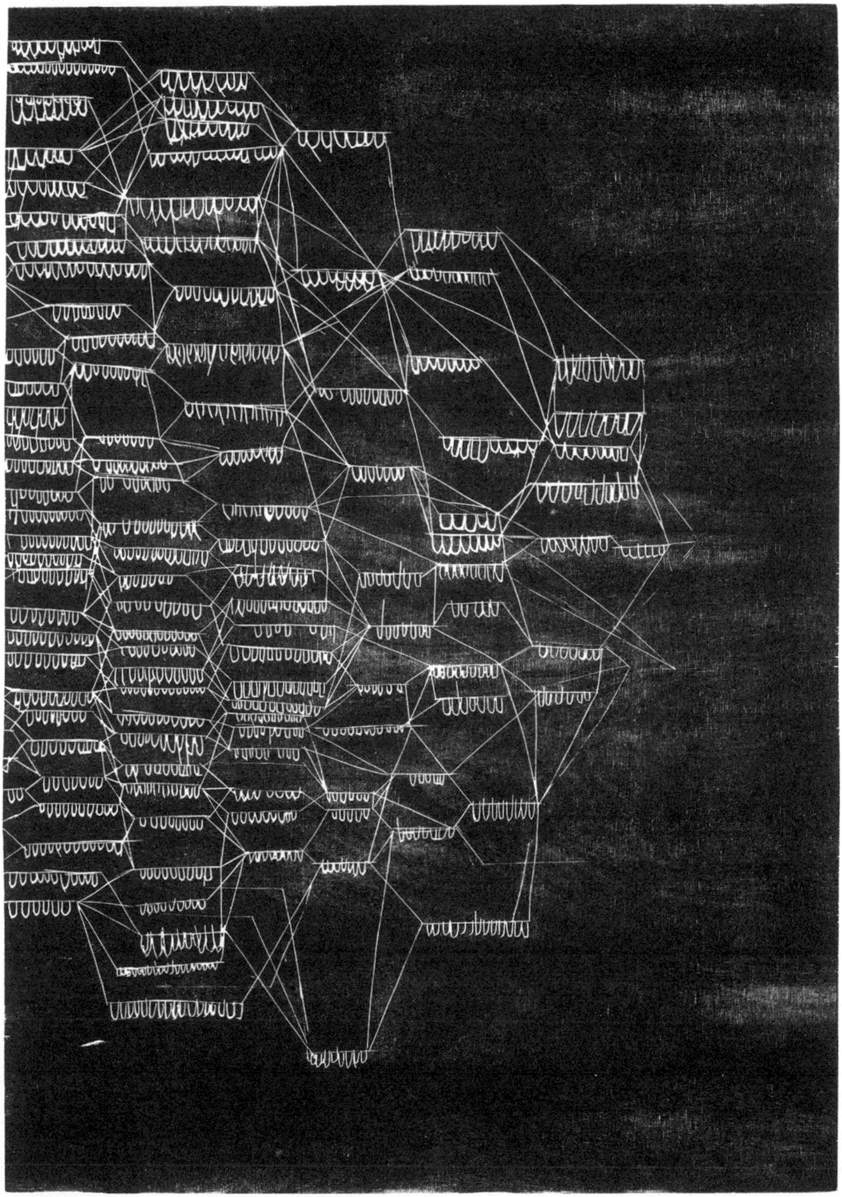

Hannah Toticki

TOUCH SCREEN PROTECTION RINGS
2019 · Wood, silver, gold-plated silver · Acquired 2020

Hannah Toticki's *Touch Screen Protection Rings* consists of silver rings meant to be worn on the index finger and thumb—the fingers that most often move over various screens—and are supposed to prevent the use of mobile phones. The rings encourage a focus on being present 'here and now' instead of being in a variety of other digital spaces and relationships. Toticki's work moves in the borderlands between art, industrial design, fashion, and theater. It raises questions about what happens when responsibility is shifted from the collective to the individual and makes us aware of our physical relationships to technology and economics. Using humor, she takes on subjects that can be perceived as dry and difficult; through objects, performances, and lectures, she depicts connections between the global and personal exhaustion, working life as a possible secular religion, and the ability to rest in a society that constantly strives for productivity.

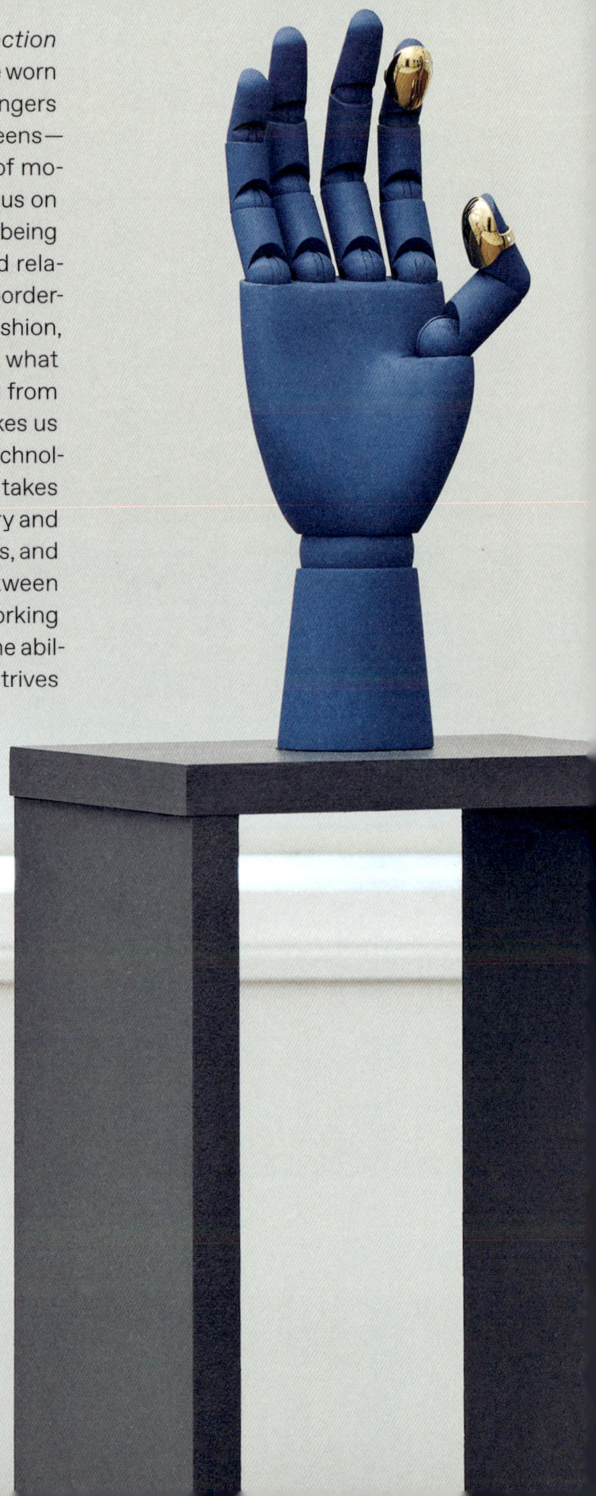

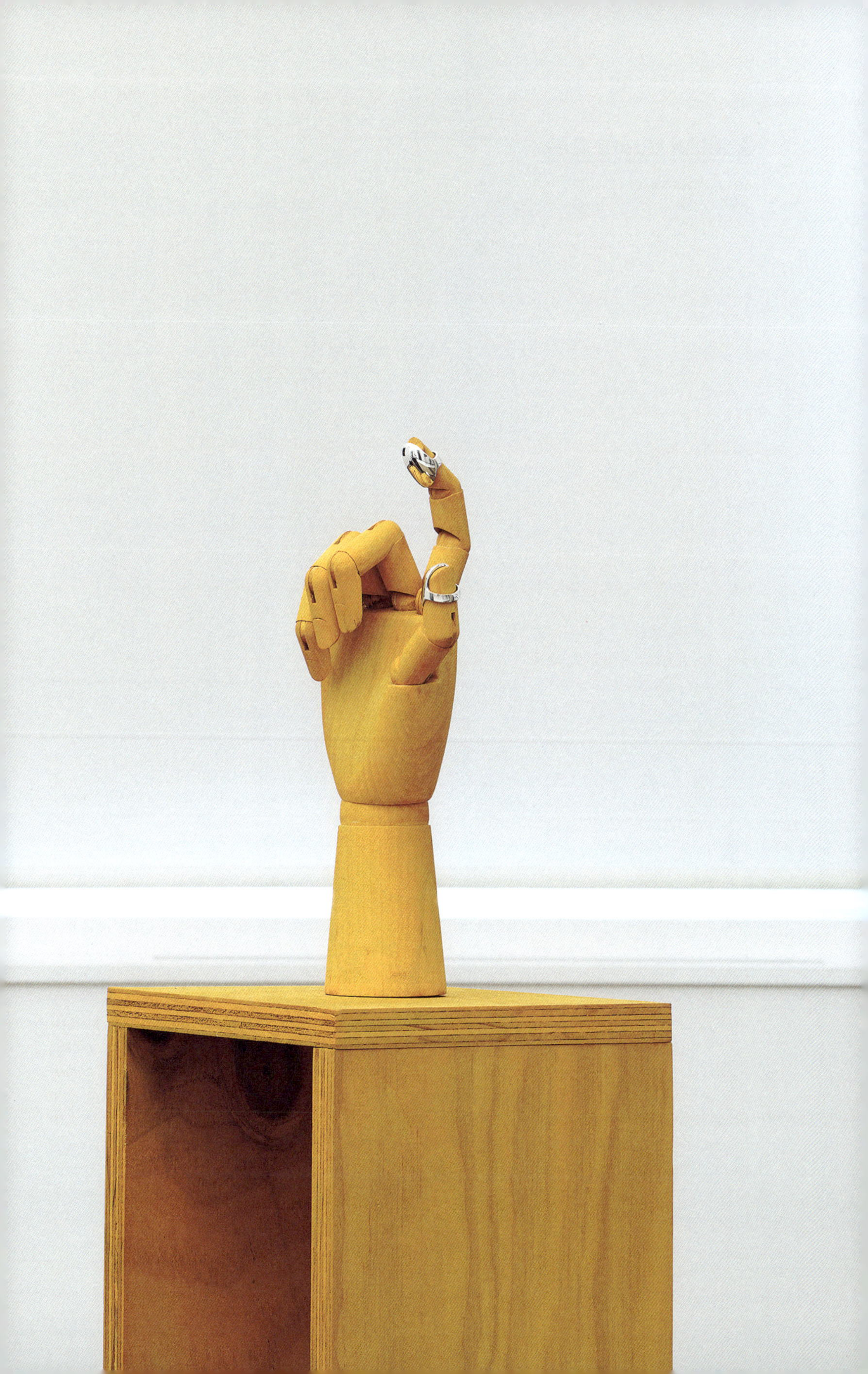

Adelita Husni-Bey

AFTER THE FINISH LINE

2015 · Video (12:53 min) · Courtesy of the artist & Laveronica arte contemporanea

In the video work *After the Finish Line*, we meet a group of young top athletes who have all suffered injuries as a result of their practice. Here, conversations about what it means to race and compete are interwoven with personal experiences of pain and failure, and where their desire for success comes from. The film's mode alternates between the aesthetic approach of sports brand advertising, where the young people are presented as perfect machines, and a more experimental documentary appeal, where the artist makes visible how the young people, after their injuries, experience psychological breakdowns. In the film, sports operate as a metaphor for life. Being a top athlete is like being the 'perfect' human being, especially in an American context, where the athletic ideal is deeply rooted in the notion of success.

Artist and researcher Adelita Husni-Bey has a background in sociology and engages in questions that, among other things, relate to the mechanisms behind political and economic power and control. In her role as an artist, she strives to provide a reflection on how Western society is structured and works to create alternatives to the status quo.

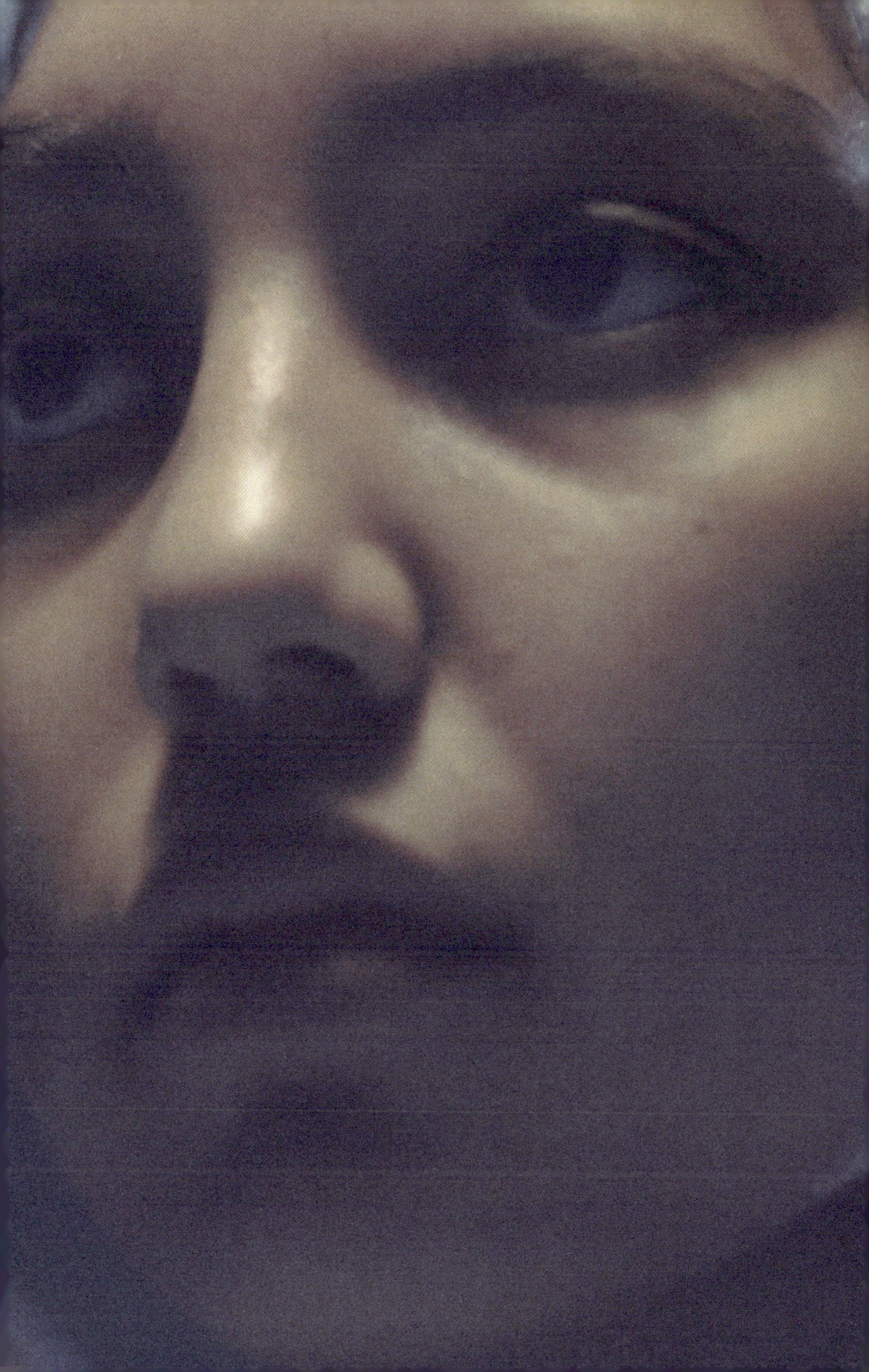

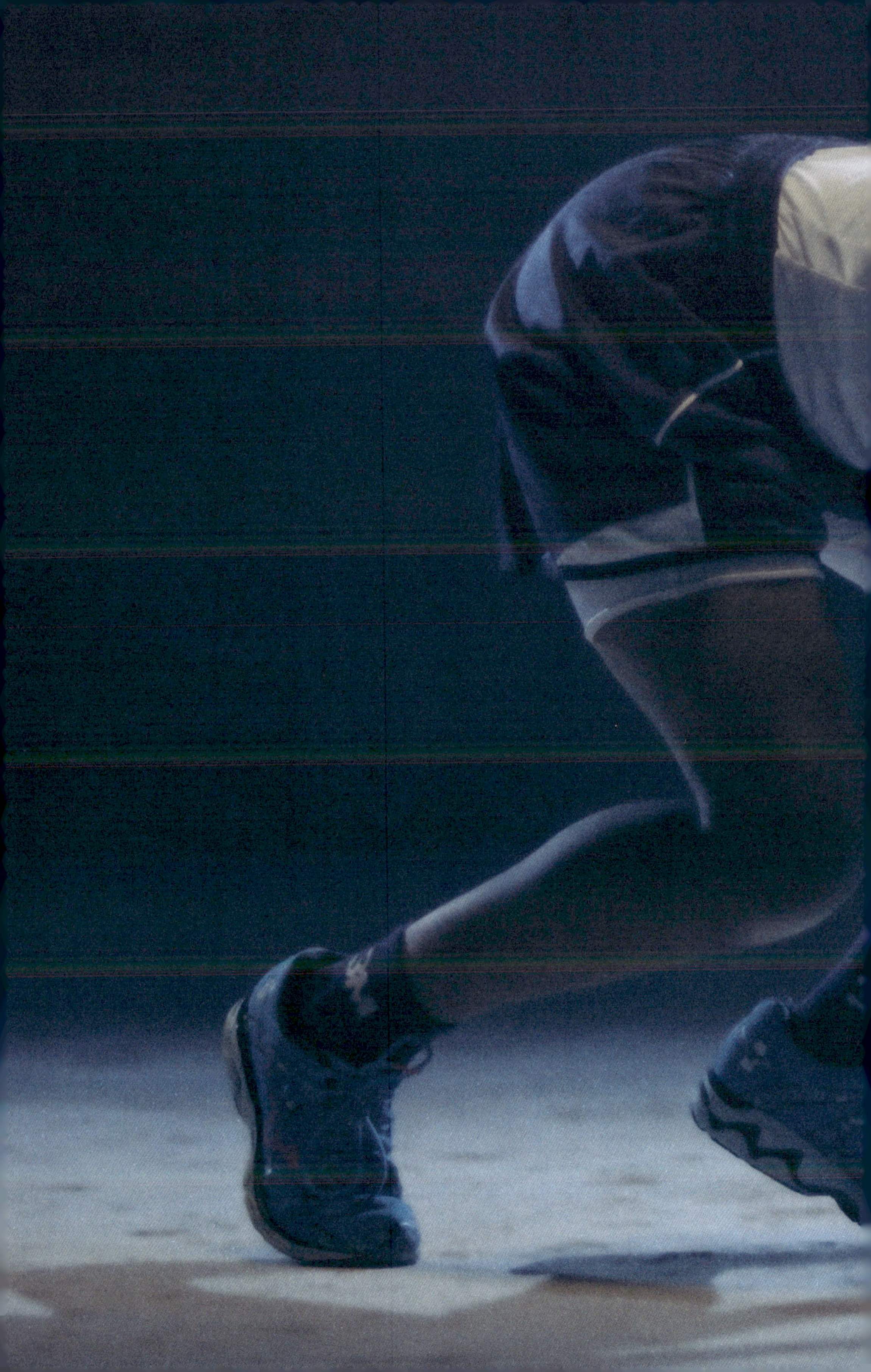

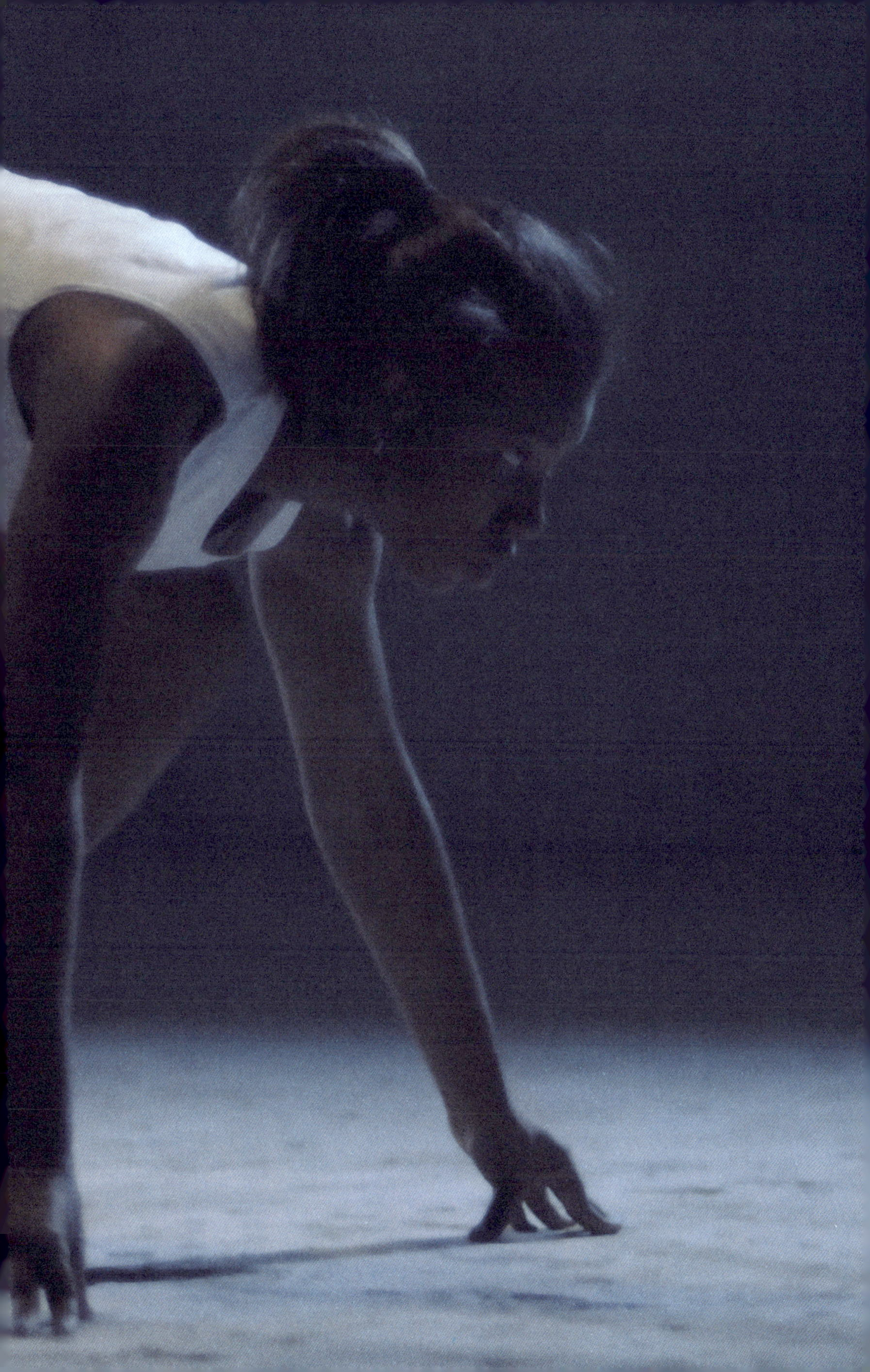

Anita Christoffersson

MÄTA—DUGA (MEASURE—SUFFICE)
2001 · Tablecloth, embroidery · Acquired 2022

Anita Christoffersson divides her artistry into three branches: meditation, materiality, and existential works. The piece *Mäta—duga* (Measure—Suffice [p. 51, detail]) belongs to the latter category and portrays the anguish humanity lives with and examines what it means to be human. The words 'measure' (mäta) and 'suffice' (duga) are embroidered over and over, one after the other, on a woven linen tablecloth—one of countless objects that Christoffersson inherited from her mother. The work deals with the relationship between mother and daughter, not living up to expectations regarding family and career choices, but can also be seen from a wider societal perspective where measurability has become the norm. *Mäta—duga* (Measure—Suffice) gives shape to despair and sadness, but also invites new conversations and perspectives. The work illustrates the enormous significance that everyday objects can have for our interior landscape and how they are intertwined with people and emotions.

duga

mäta

duga

mäta

duga

E.B. Itso

WE RESIST THEREFORE WE EXIST
2015–21 · Inkjet prints, frames made of wood from a now demolished occupied house · Acquired 2023

THE BLUE ROOM (SNAKE RIVER CORRECTIONAL INSTITUTION)
2017 · Video installation · Acquired 2023

The video installation *The Blue Room (Snake River Correctional Institution)* (pp. 54–57) is a reconstruction of a cell called 'The Blue Room' at a prison in Oregon where inmates are encouraged to spend their daily 40 minutes outside the isolation cell. 'The Blue Room' is part of a research project that investigates whether images of nature can calm inmates and make them less violent. E.B. Itso's work illustrates the paradoxical reality that the inmates face, as there is evidence that isolation is in itself a form of psychological torture that increases the individual's propensity for violence.

Cutting oneself off from society and creating alternative communities on one's own terms is depicted in *We Resist Therefore We Exist* (p. 53). The series consists of photographs taken from inside an occupied building in Copenhagen and captures windows that have been covered with elaborate wooden structures by the residents to protect both themselves and their housing from the police. Here, autonomy is pitted against daylight and acts of resistance take physical form.

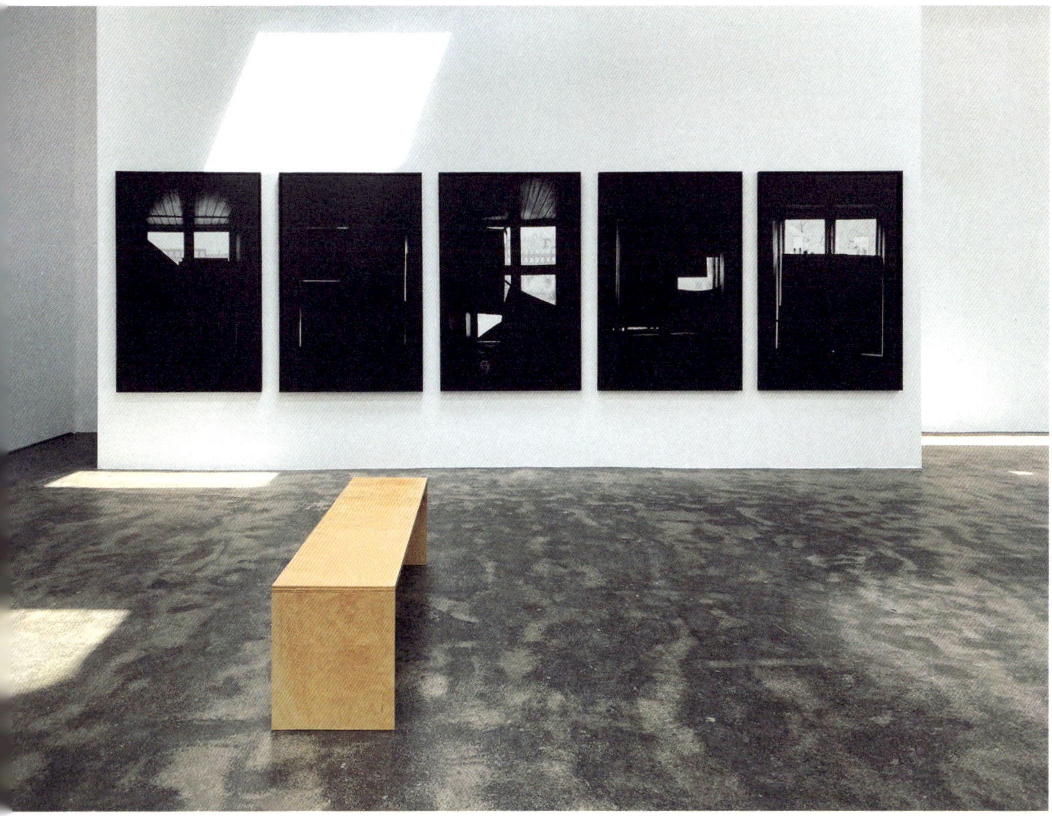

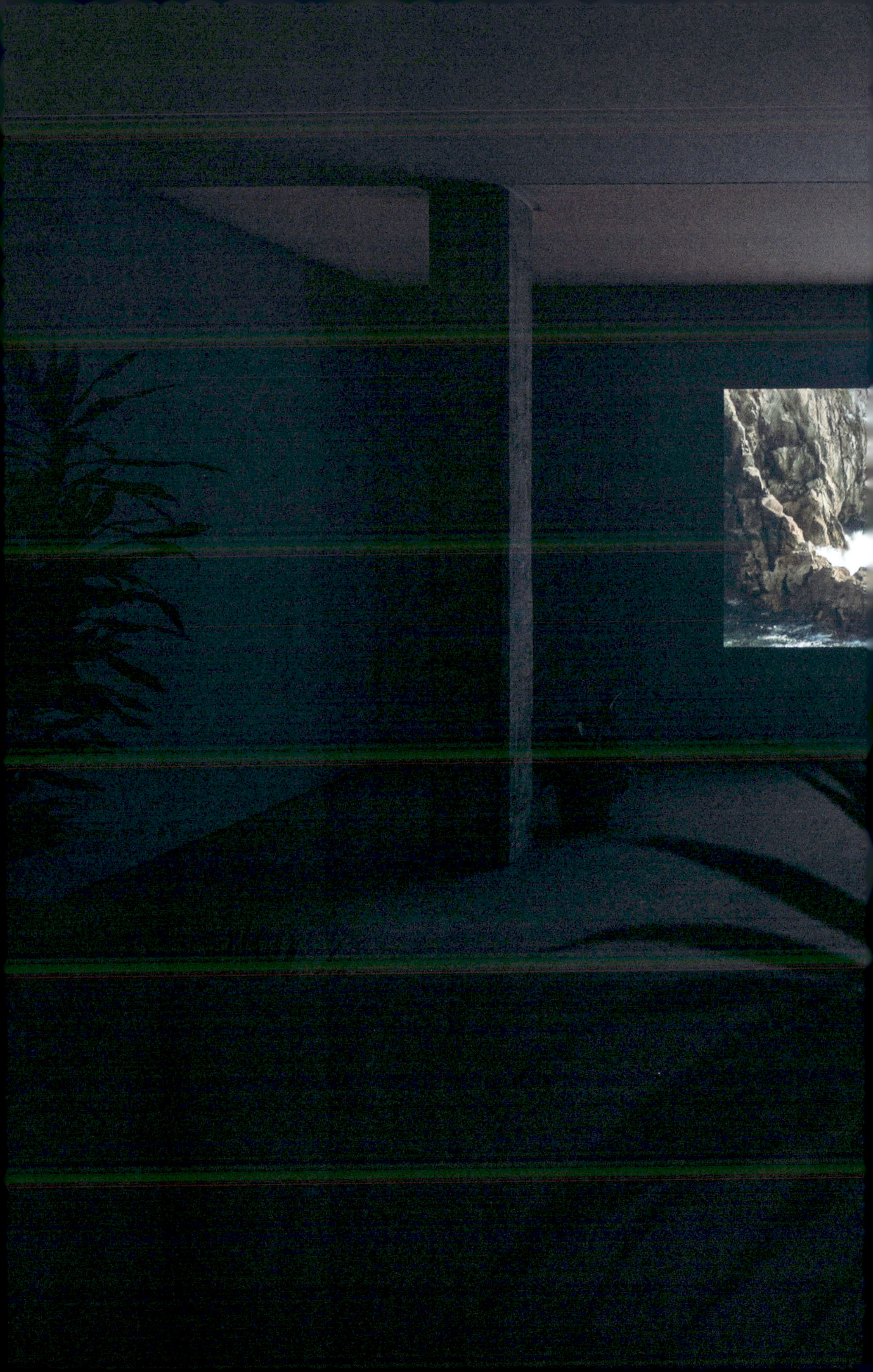

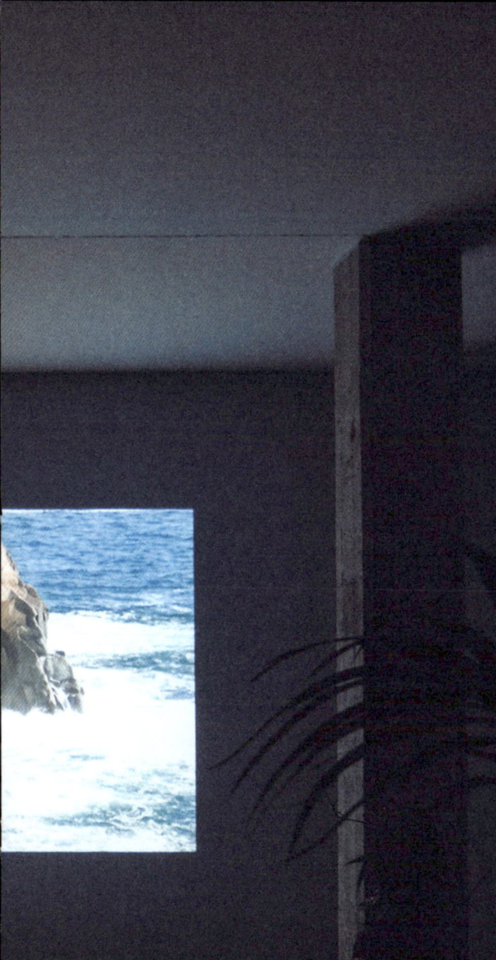

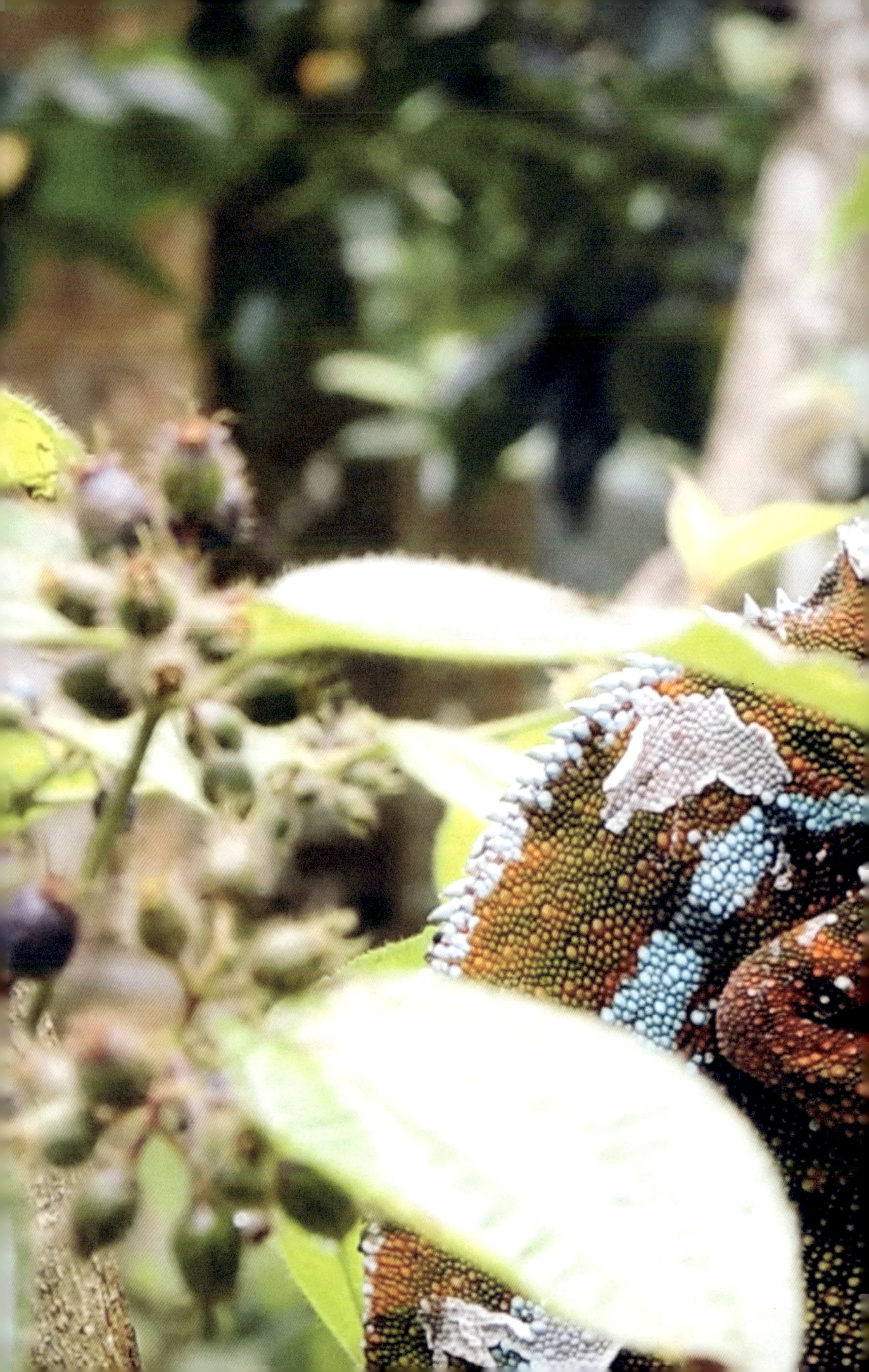

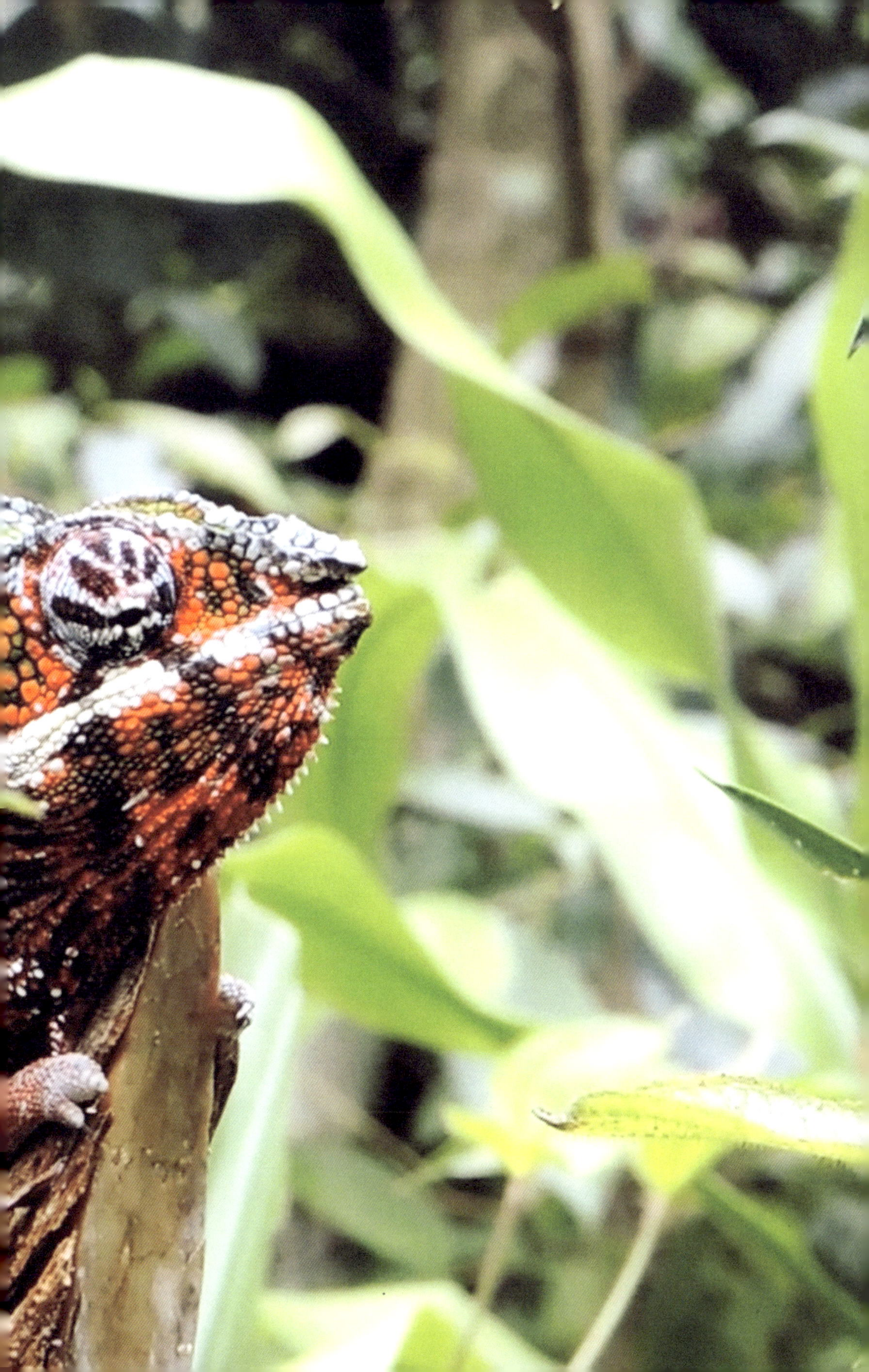

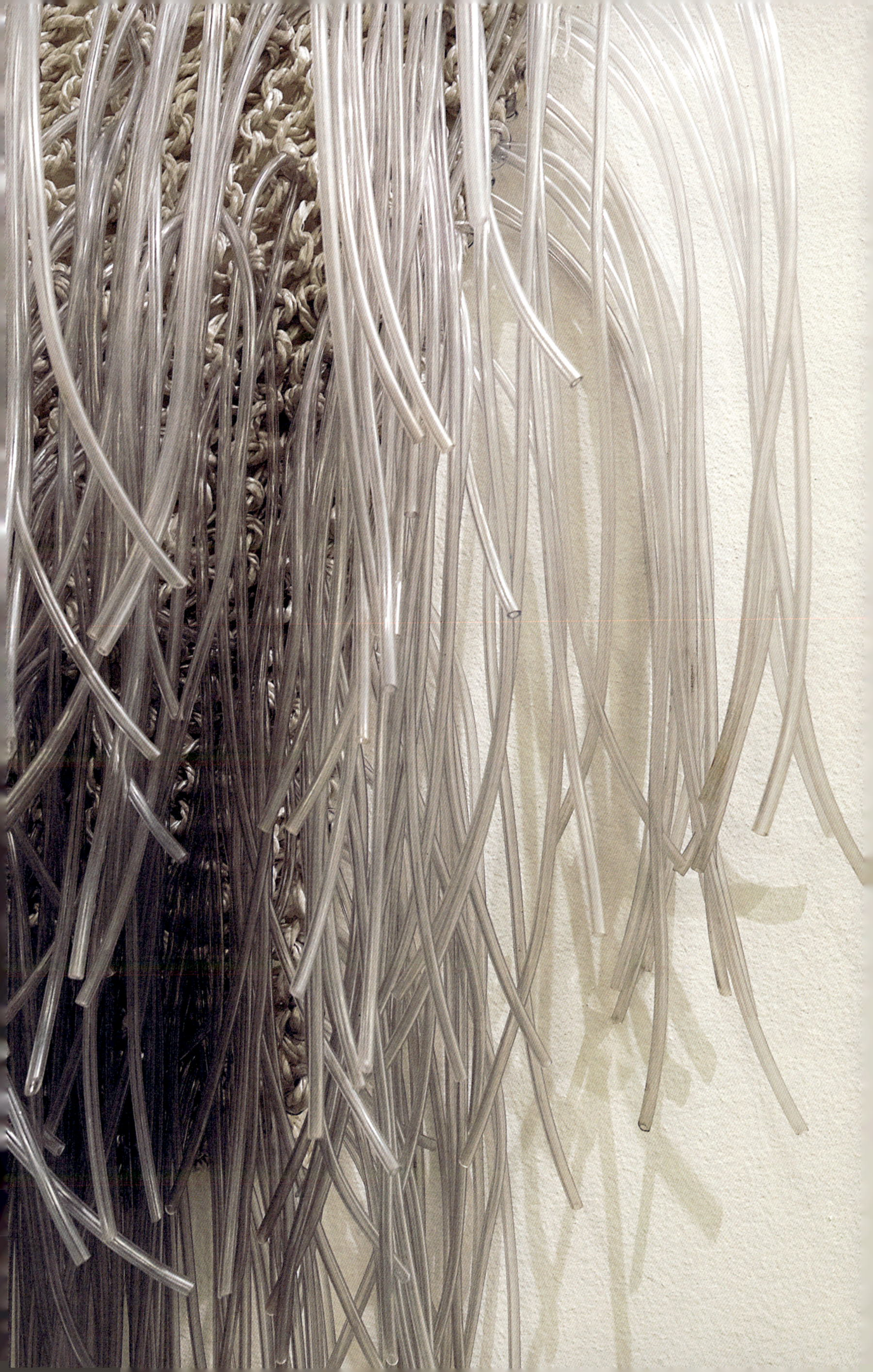

Leif Holmstrand

CARPET
1998 · Washing line, PVC hose · Acquired 2008

Leif Holmstrand's multifaceted practice touches on human vulnerability and needs, and moves freely between subjects such as rituals, violence, and transgressive gender affiliations. The work *Carpet* is designed as a long-pile rug and is made of PVC hose. The material is associated more closely with sterilized health care or industry than the sphere of the home, where the carpet is often used to evoke warmth, comfort, and care. Here, the characteristic and paradoxical duality of Holmstrand's art is brought to the fore; the familiar carpet with its connotations instead evokes a plastic organism which can seem both disgusting and repulsive. In its complexity, the work shows that human beings are not either/or, but that everything is contained within the same body. With empathy and understanding for humanity, she is allowed to be both beautiful and repulsive.

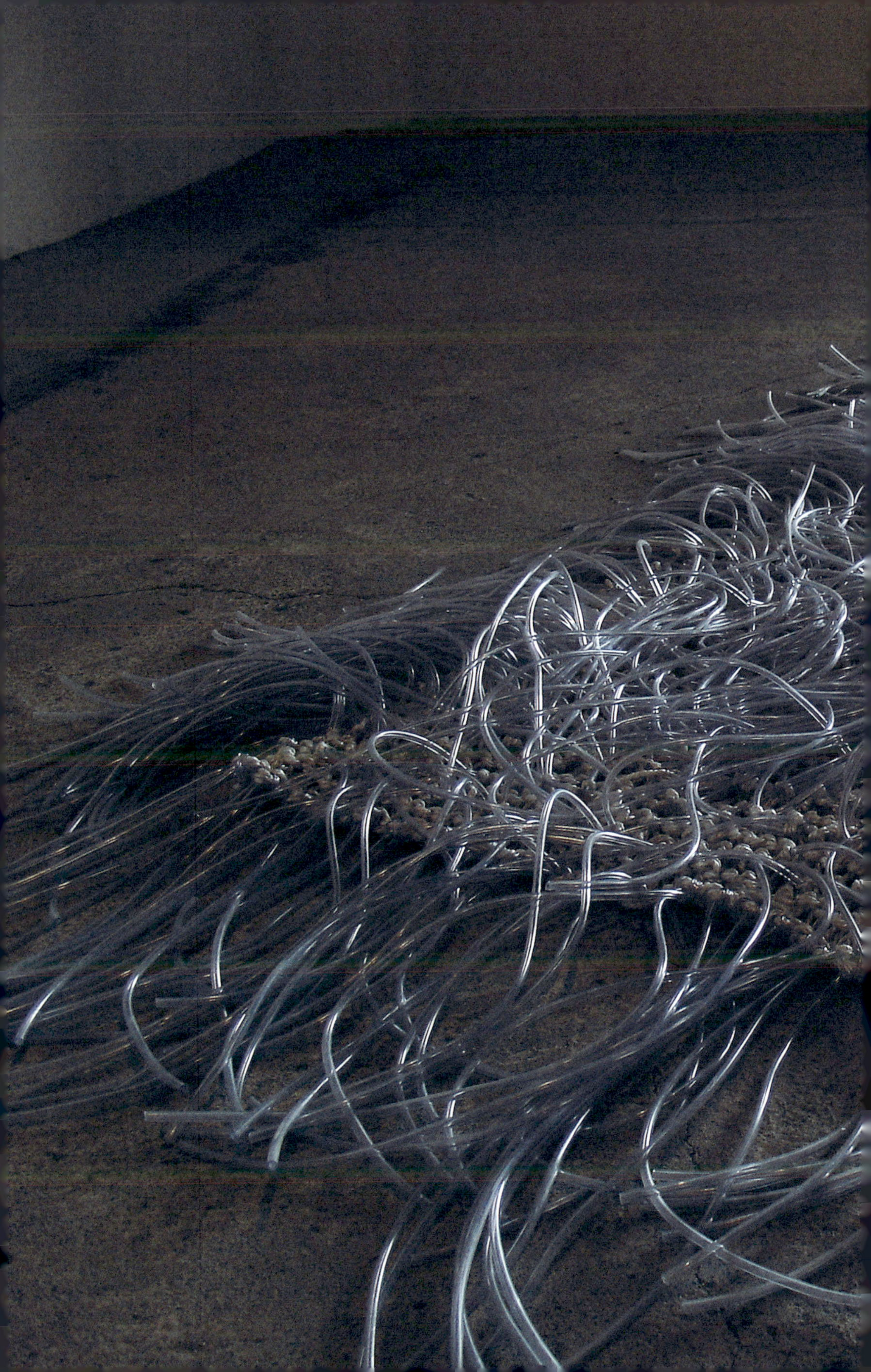

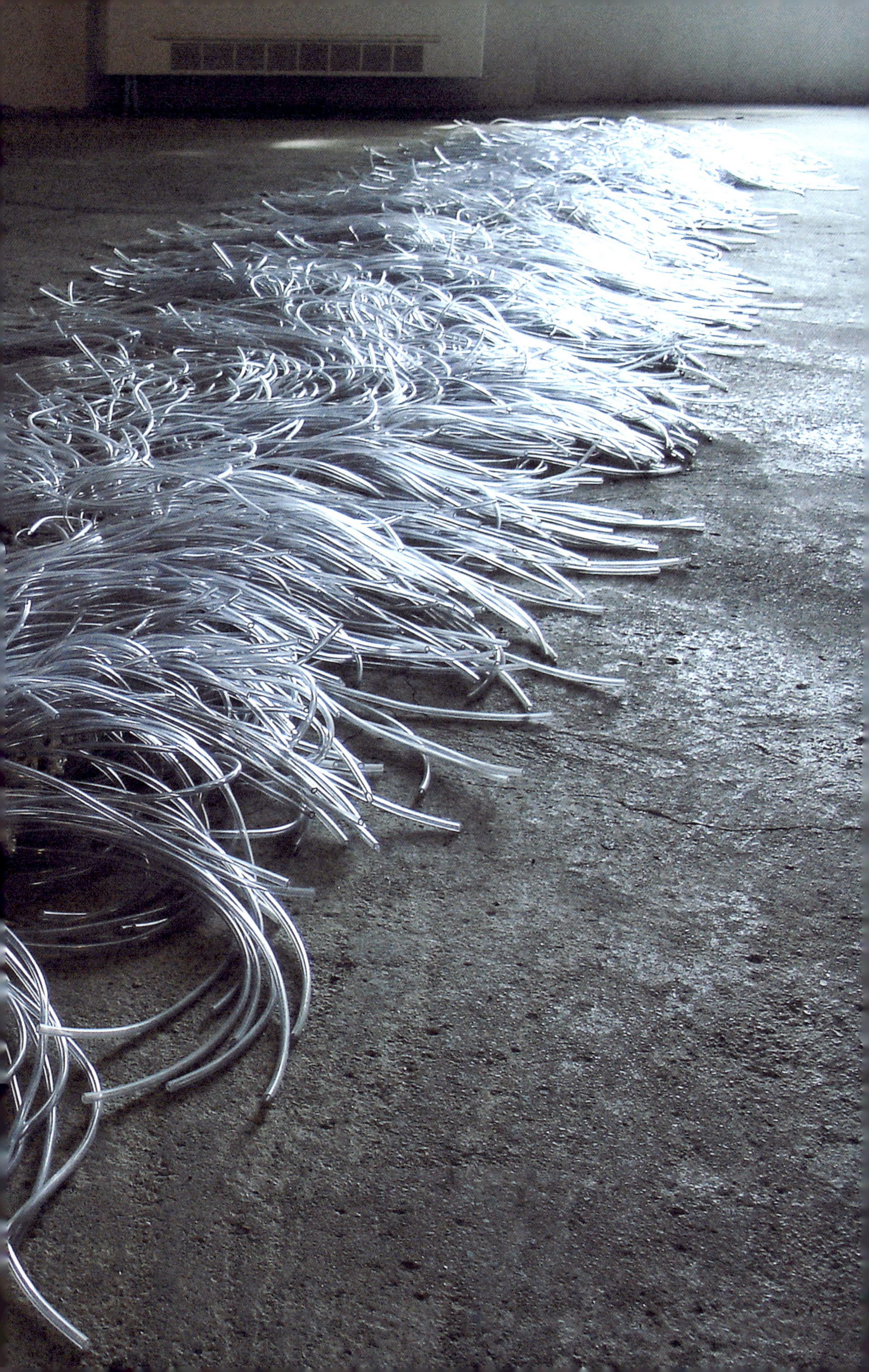

Helena Fernández-Cavada

LOOKING FOR A STATE OF HARMONY, ALTHOUGH THERE IS TENSION TO BE RELEASED
2022–23 · Watercolor and ink on paper · Acquired 2023

Can art offer a place for stillness, harmony, and calm? With that question, Helena Fernández-Cavada invites reflections on the meaning of art for us, both as individuals and as a collective. The question may seem to refer to something truly desirable, while it may at the same time be perceived as pretentious and somewhat impossible. The title—*Looking for a State of Harmony, Although There Is Tension to Be Released*—also expresses these contradictions.

Fernández-Cavada has long worked with performances and participatory projects that address how art can contribute to greater social well-being. In this work, she shifts perspective to explore how the aesthetic experience can provide opportunity for individual introspection and existential well-being. The drawings are produced using a method whereby everything must be in place and present in the moment—mind, soul, body, space, and light—so that the entire work can be carried out in one continuous flow without distraction or interruption. The series can be seen as the embodiment of a state of absolute harmony while also harboring an inherent hope that it will contaminate its surroundings.

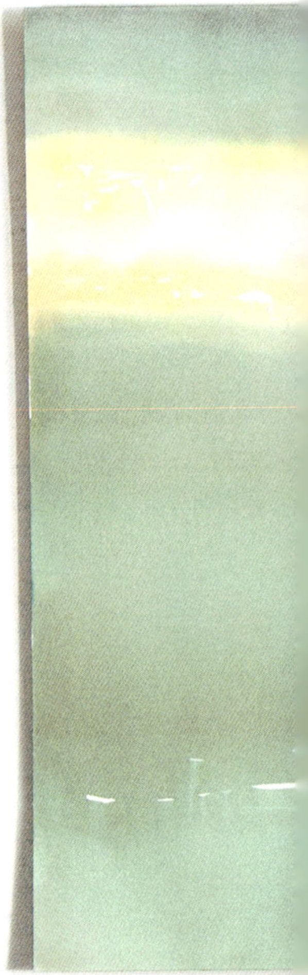

Britt-Ingrid Persson BIP

PÅ FRUSET VATTEN—MEMBRAN (ON FROZEN WATER—MEMBRANE)
1980s · Concrete, Styrofoam, graphite powder patination · Donation 2020

PÅ FRUSET VATTEN—SLAGRUTA (ON FROZEN WATER—DOWSING ROD)
1980s · Concrete, Styrofoam · Donation 2020

In the 1980s, Britt-Ingrid Persson BIP made a number of works with the title *På fruset vatten* (On Frozen Water). All the sculptures in the series consist of twins, which she interpreted as two sides of herself. In *På fruset vatten—slagruta* (On Frozen Water—Dowsing Rod [pp. 68–69]), the figures each hold a dowsing rod, a pseudoscientific tool that has been used to sense the presence of what we cannot see, for example in the search for water, energies, or minerals. Here, the dowsing rod can be understood as a search for knowledge—about oneself and the world that surrounds us. In *På fruset vatten—membran* (On Frozen Water—Membrane [p. 67, detail]), one twin has been replaced with a small figure that the larger one is holding in its arms, covered by a thin membrane. The membrane can be seen as the need for protection, for our physical and mental survival, to be able to develop our identity and maintain our integrity. At the same time, it needs to be transparent and permeable so that contact with the outside world can occur.

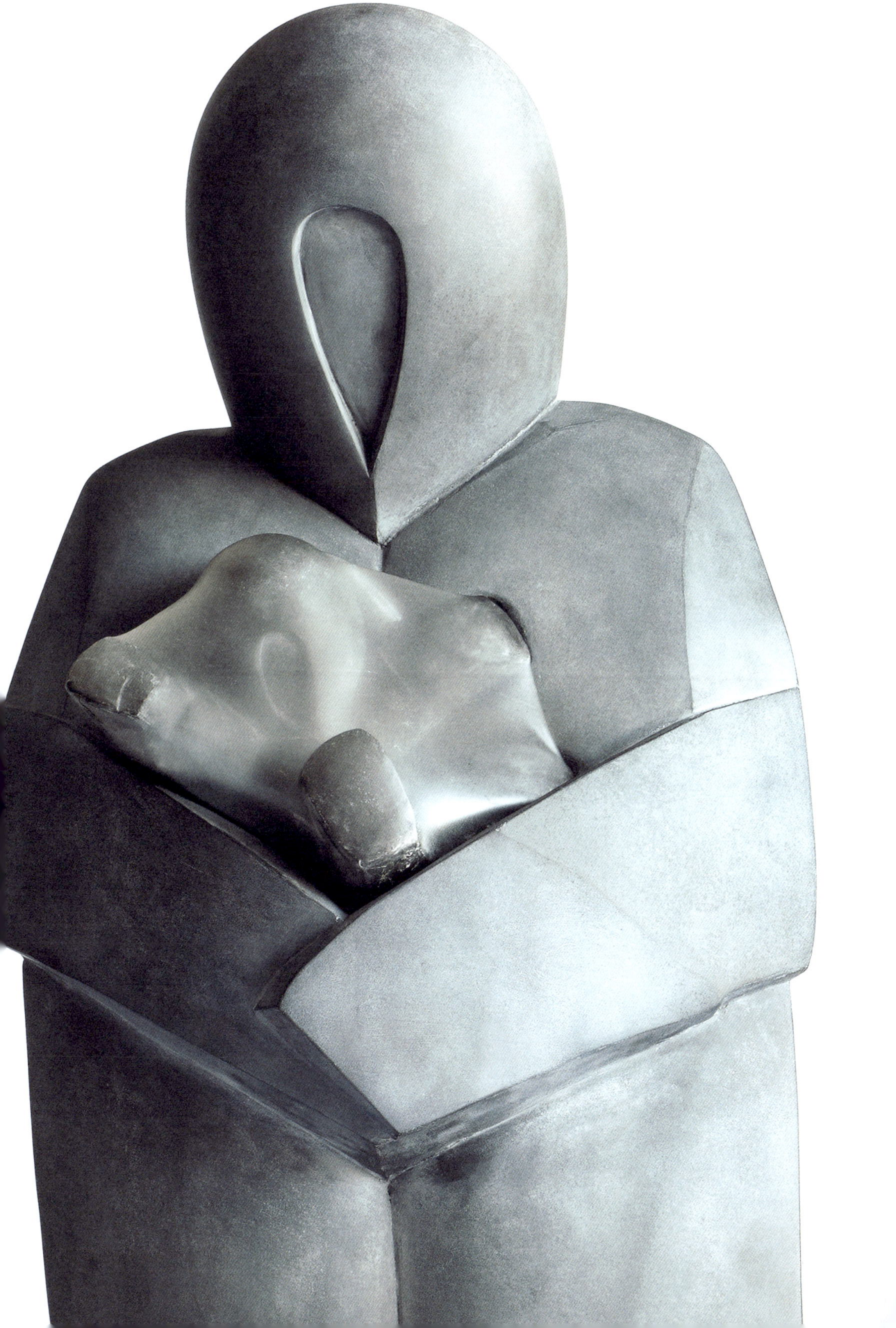

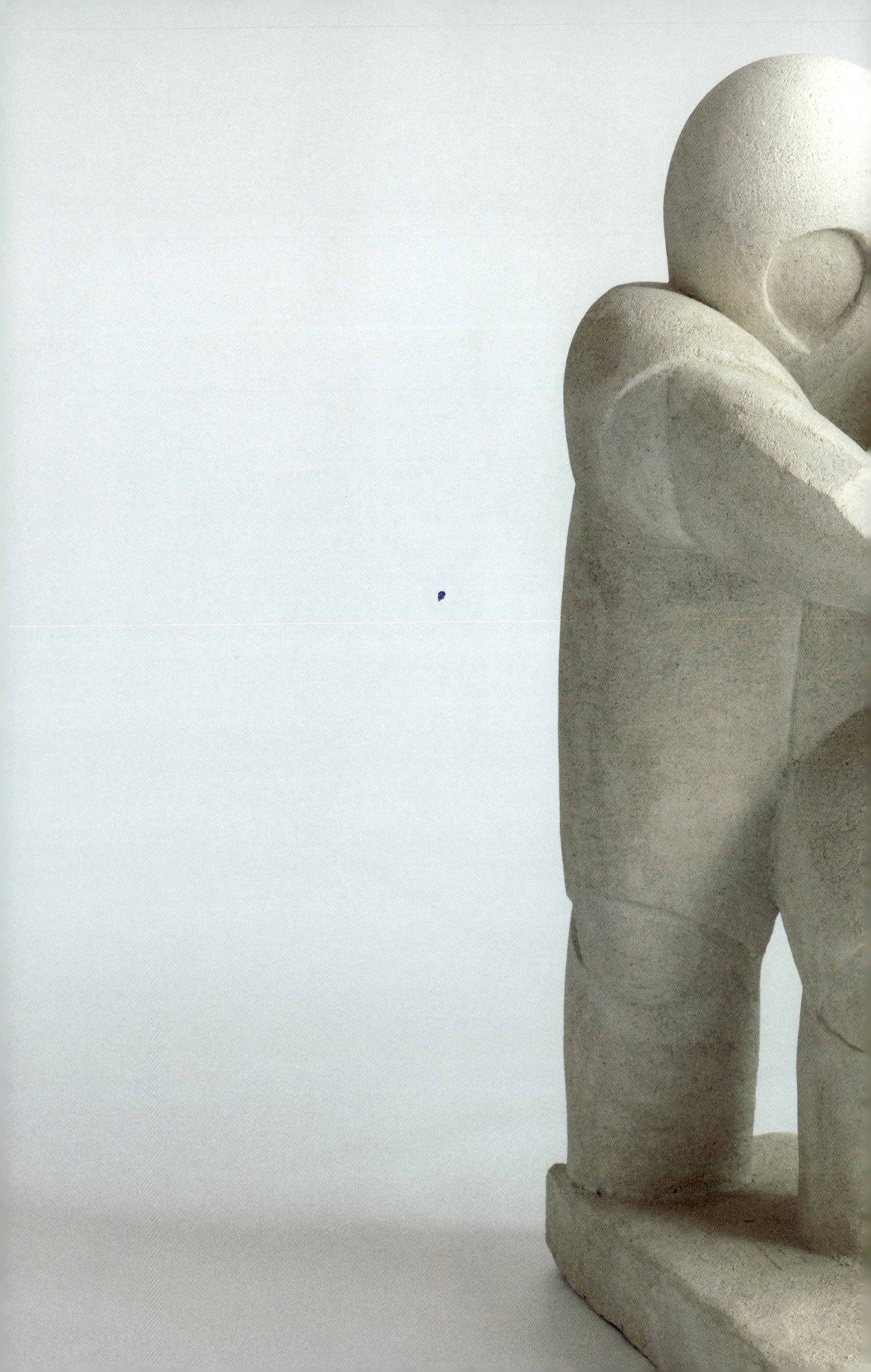

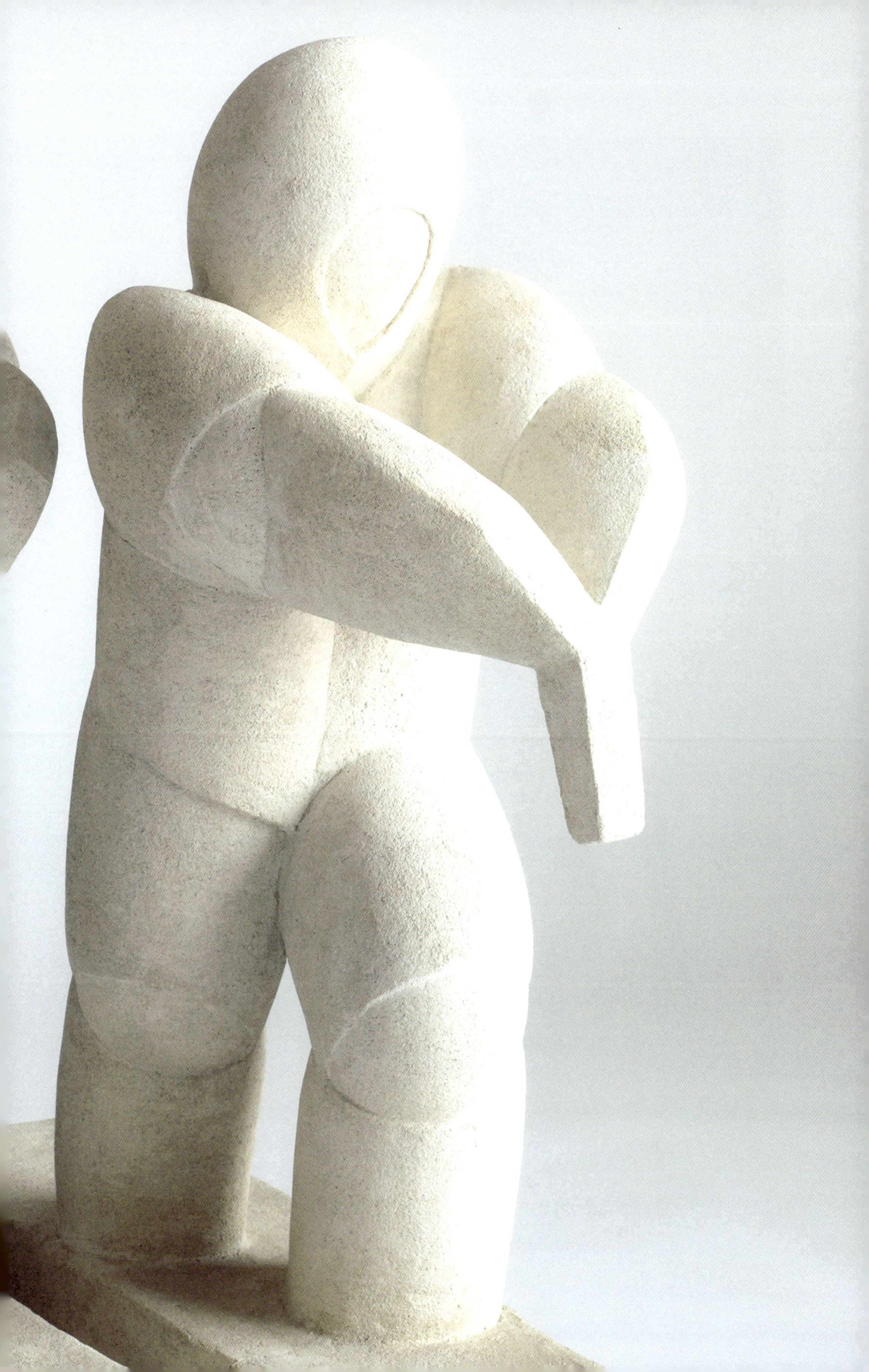

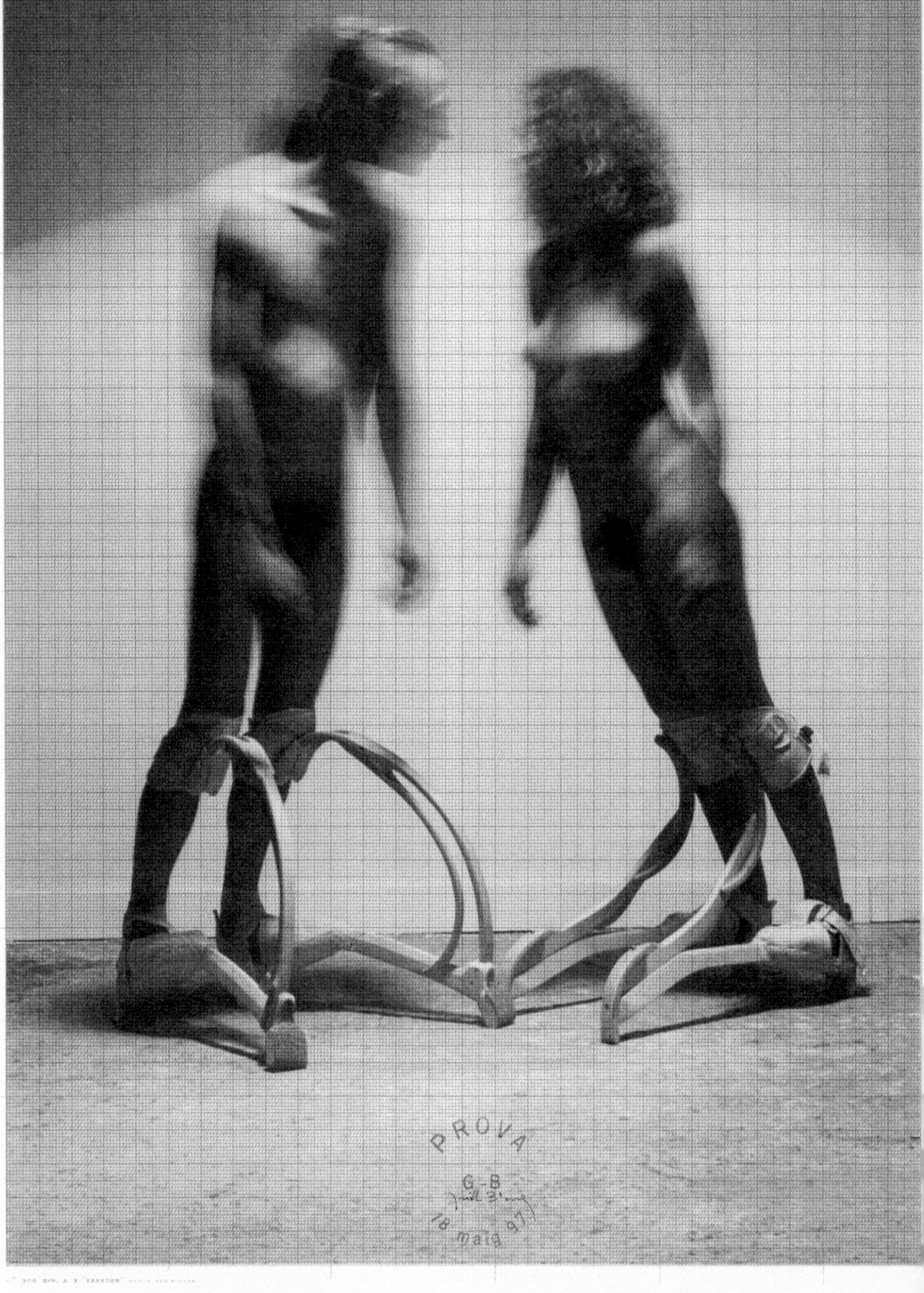
PROVA
G-B
18 maio 97

Ramón Guillén-Balmes

MODELS FOR KLAUS AND MICHA
1997 · Felt, wood, photographs, watercolor · Donation 2002

The objects in Ramón Guillén-Balmes' work *Models for Klaus and Micha* are reminiscent of prostheses or medical aids and were made for the performance artists Klaus Speis and Micha Rusch. The work is part of the series *Models to Be Titled after Tests*, where Guillén-Balmes created models specifically for people close to him who expressed a need for or lack of something, and incorporated their experiences and responses into the final result. Central to the series was the relationship between the artist and the person for whom the model was designed, and that the artwork could be utilized. On the wall above the prosthesis-like objects are photographs of how Speis and Rusch used them by strapping them onto their feet and knees, and what feelings and thoughts arose in the encounter. The terms *Vorschweben* (inclination) and *Neigung* (tilt) came to mind during the process and were incorporated into the work. Guillén-Balmes was interested in the prosthesis as an idea, as an extension of body and mind, and as a door to new perspectives.

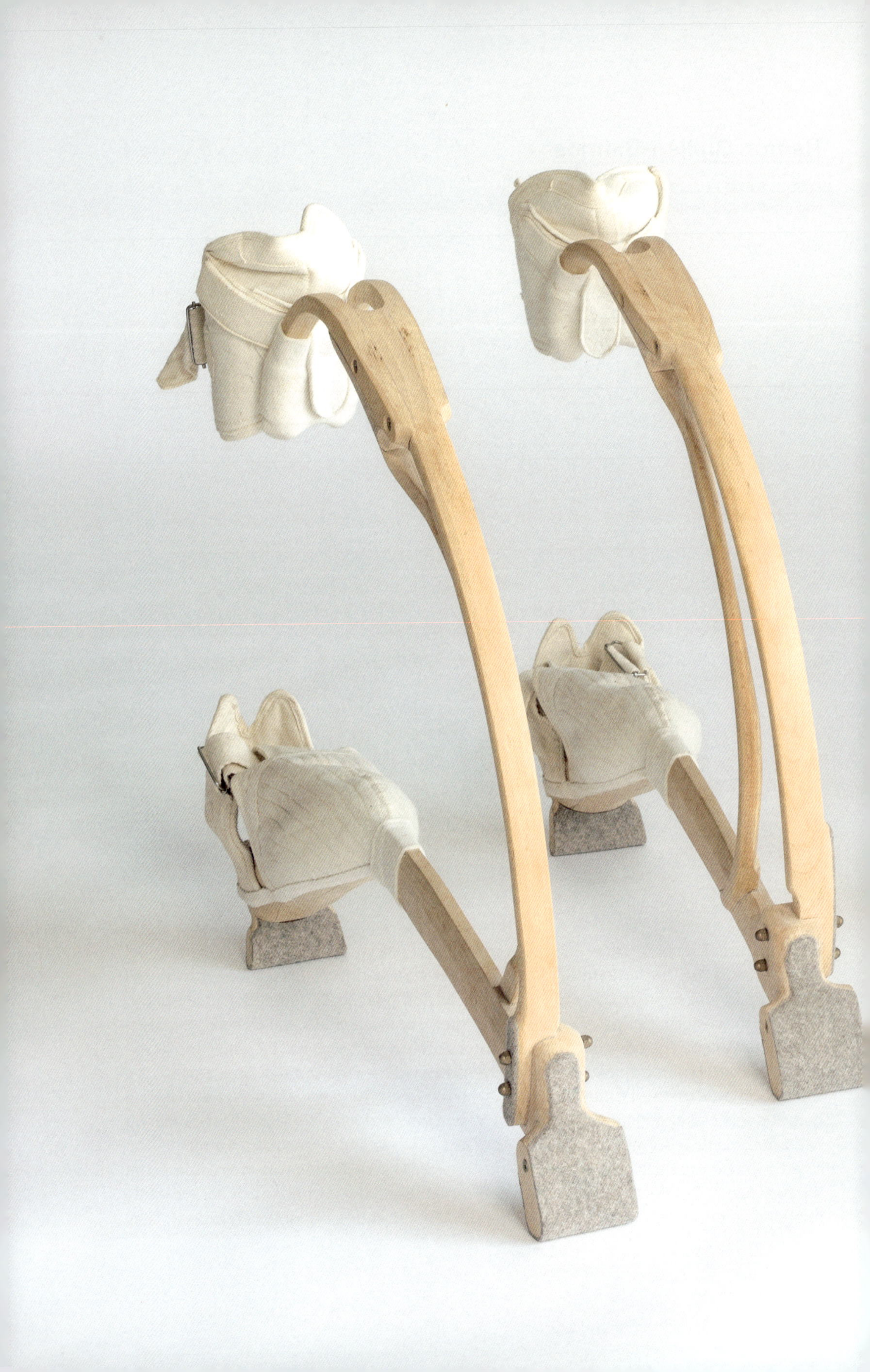

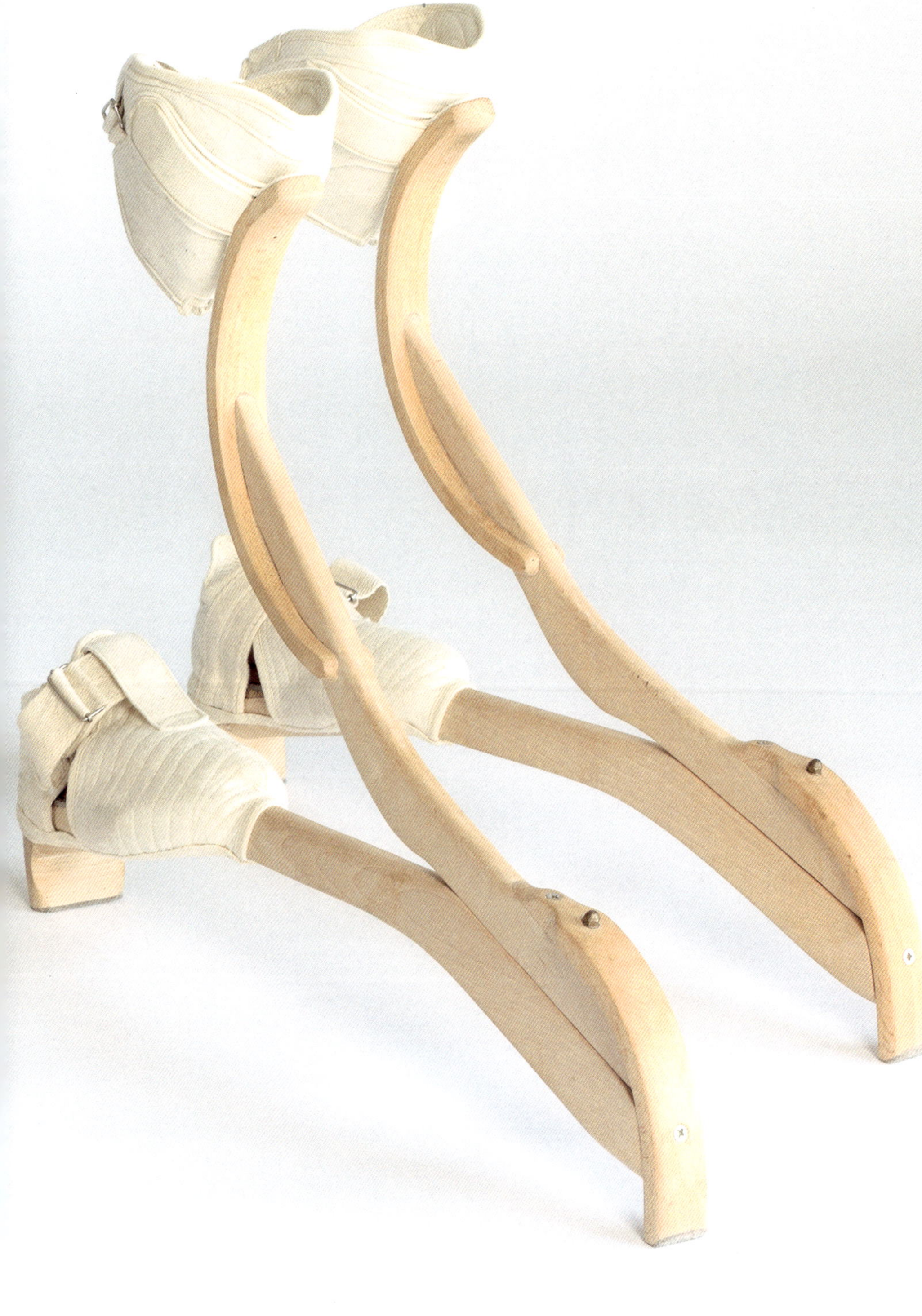

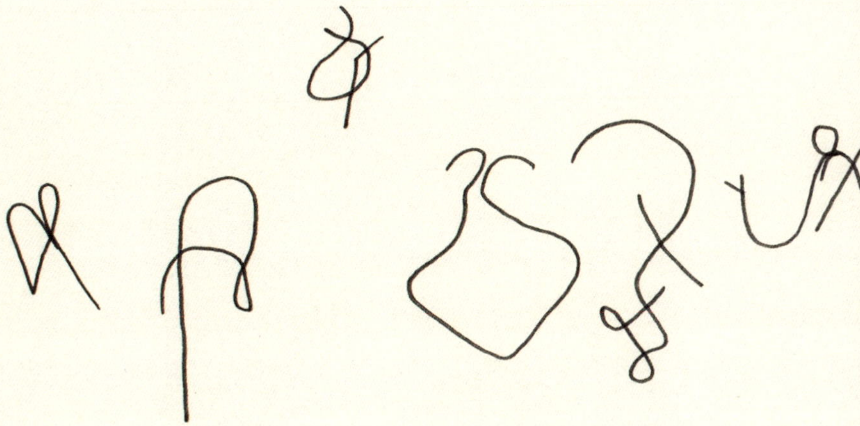

Ellinor Lager

WHITE INK NO. 23
2019 · Glazed earthenware · Acquired 2019

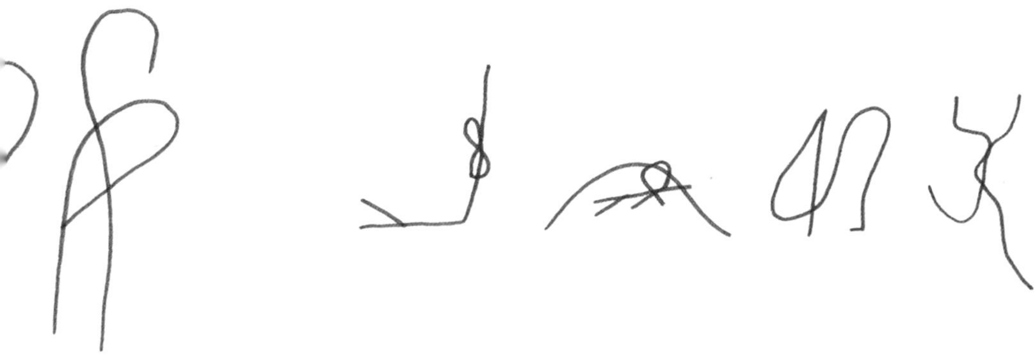

Ellinor Lager works with sculpture where experiences of life, body, and language are woven together. She sees her work as a writing with objects, where her intuitive approach allows her to articulate the realm and semiotics of the maternal body. The sculptures can be seen as translations and activations of bodily knowledge, experiences, and memories. The work *White Ink No. 23* (pp. 76–77, detail) consists of twelve characters which were first drawn with the weft she freed up by unraveling a rag rug during the end of her first pregnancy and after childbirth. 'White ink' refers to breast milk and is a term that comes from the French feminist philosopher Hélène Cixous' 1975 essay 'Le Rire de la Méduse' ('The Laugh of the Medusa'). In the same text, Cixous also coined the term *Écriture féminine* ('feminine writing') to explain the importance of women writing about themselves in order to gain an understanding of their body and self and free themselves from patriarchy. Through *White Ink No. 23*, Lager interprets Cixous' phrase and illustrates the symbiotic relationship between experience and language.

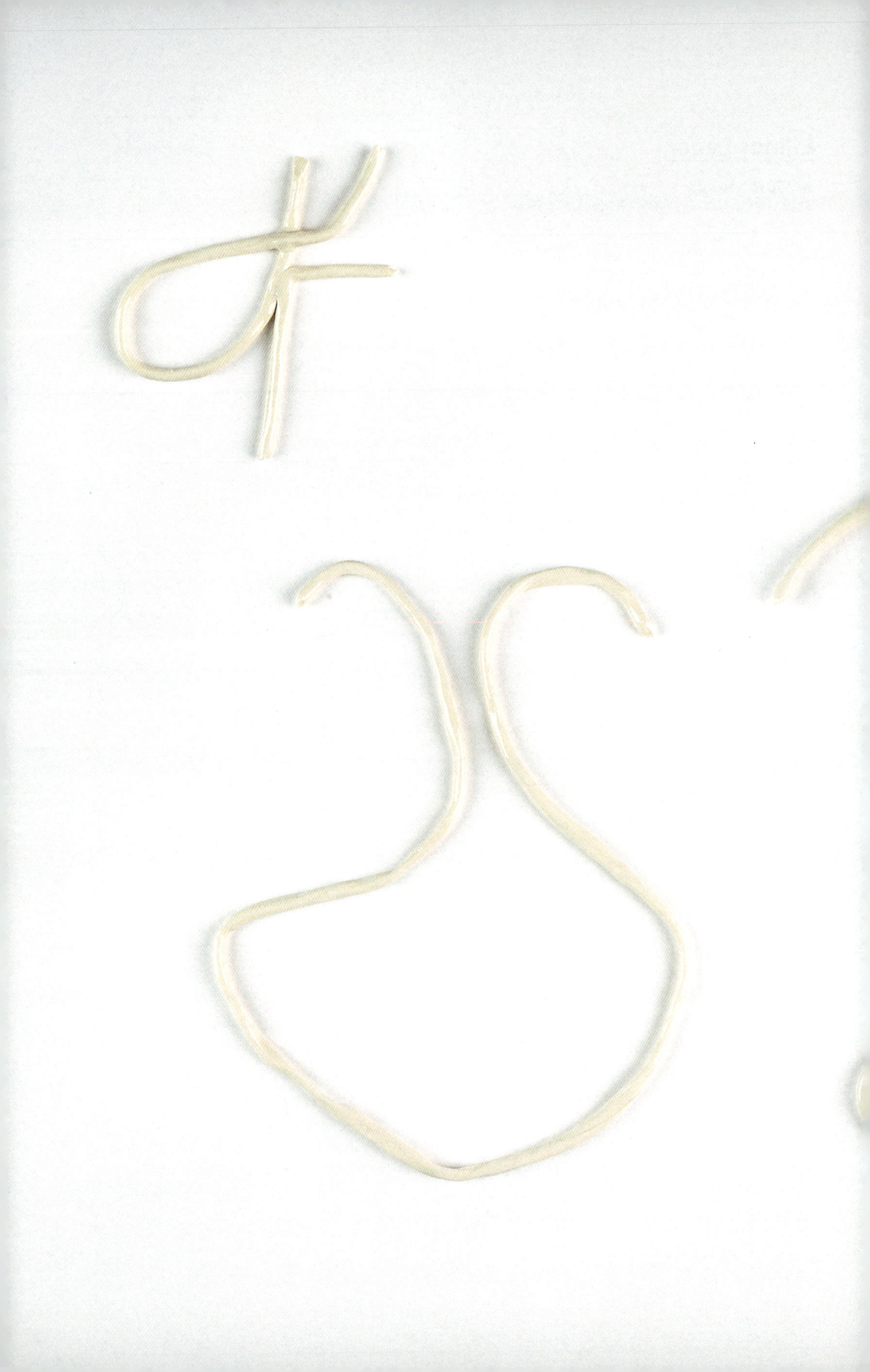

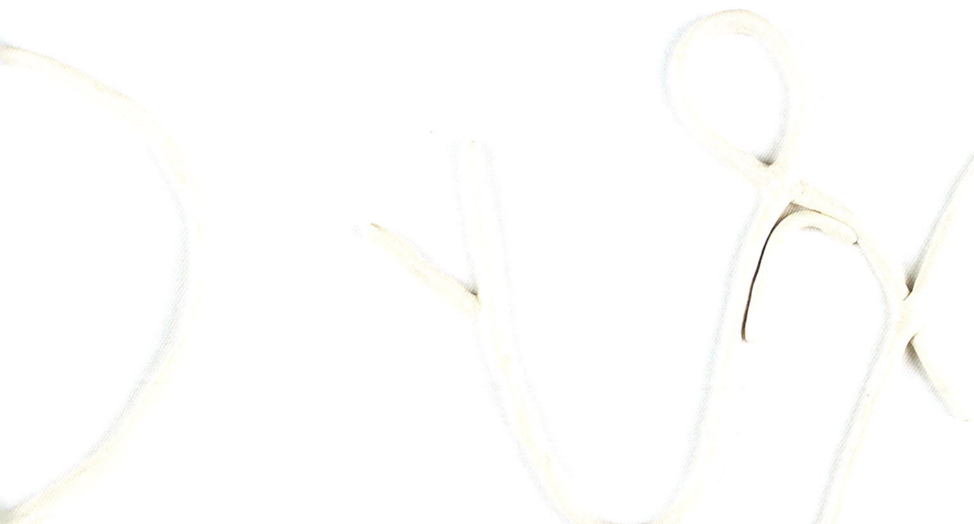

Jenny Grönvall

BECOMING ECRU

2023 · Performance and installation (oak, pine plywood and MDF) · Acquired 2023

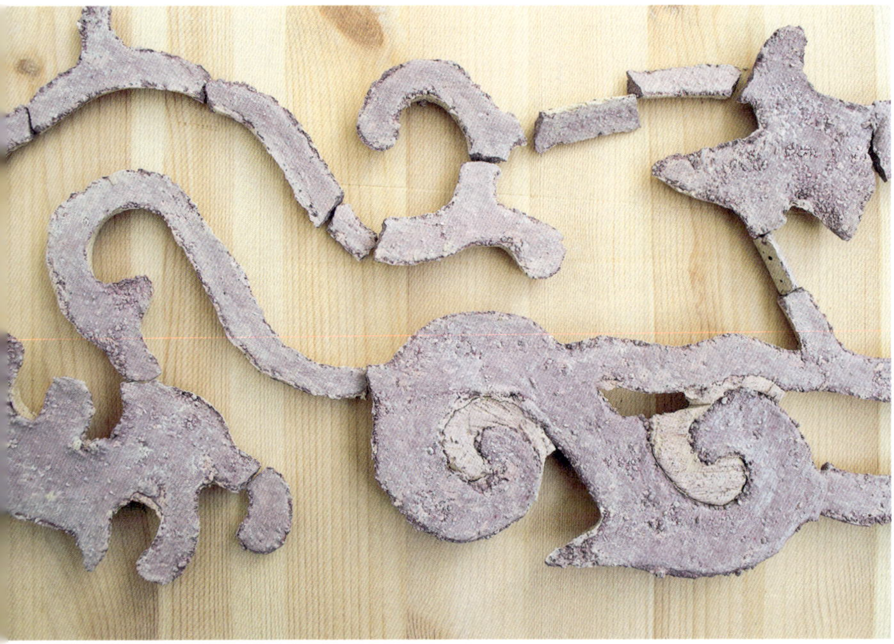

In Jenny Grönvall's sculptures, installations, and performances, the social and interpersonal are used as material to highlight and overturn affective connections. Grönvall addresses our need for belonging and how aesthetics are used in identity-creating processes and in relation to class. *becoming ecru* is an installation and a performance where she, in a New Age transformation process, charges objects with energies and invokes higher powers to achieve, for example, wealth and abundance. The work is a further extension of *The Abundance Show* (2020) and shows how notions of taste and quality emerge and how we project happiness and unhappiness onto objects, surfaces, and colors. In a previous work—*Inredning och affekt* (Interior Design and Affect [2017])—the audience was invited to the artist's home for a display of her interior design and its connection to emotions and politics.

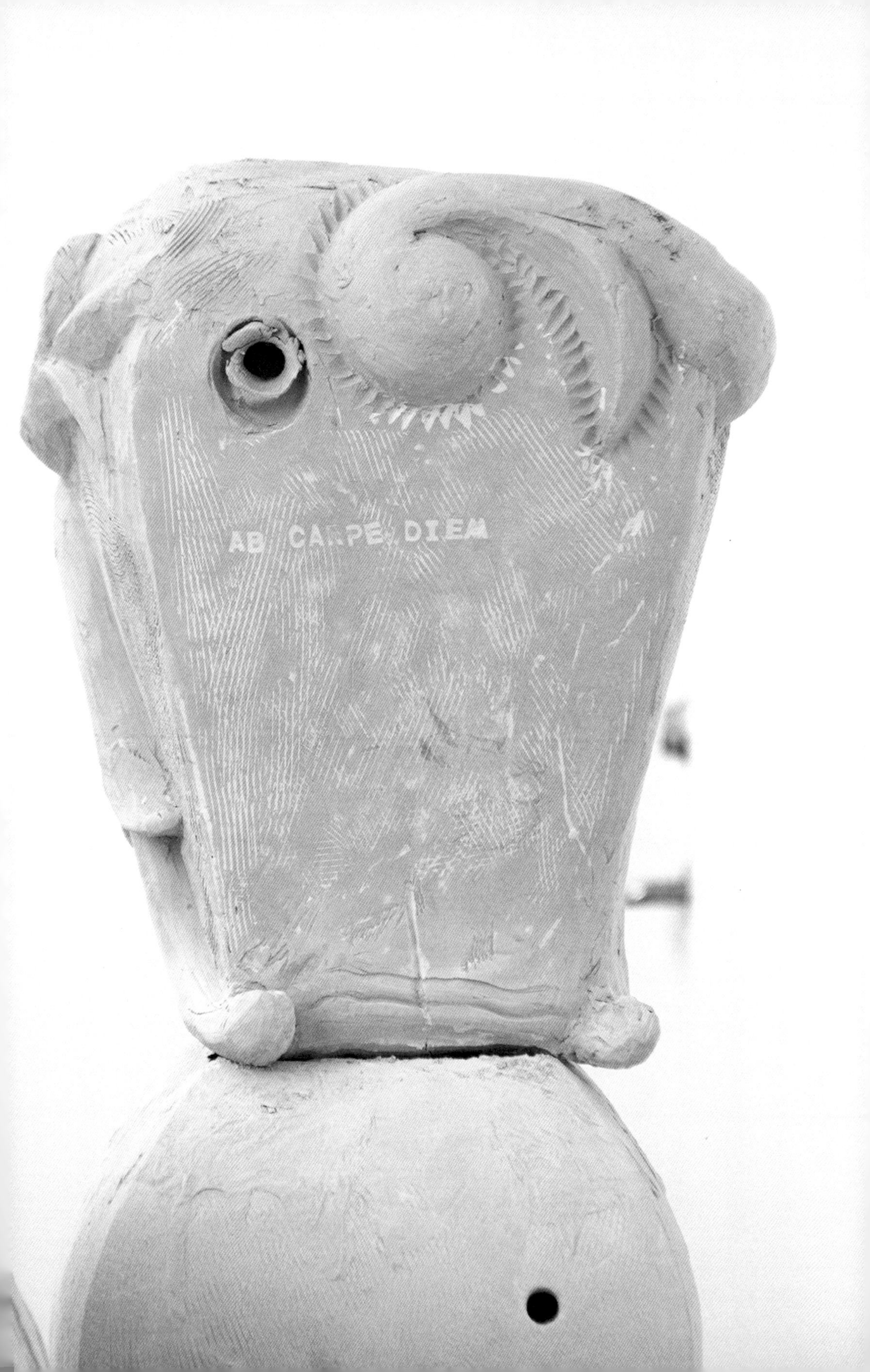
AB CARPE DIEM

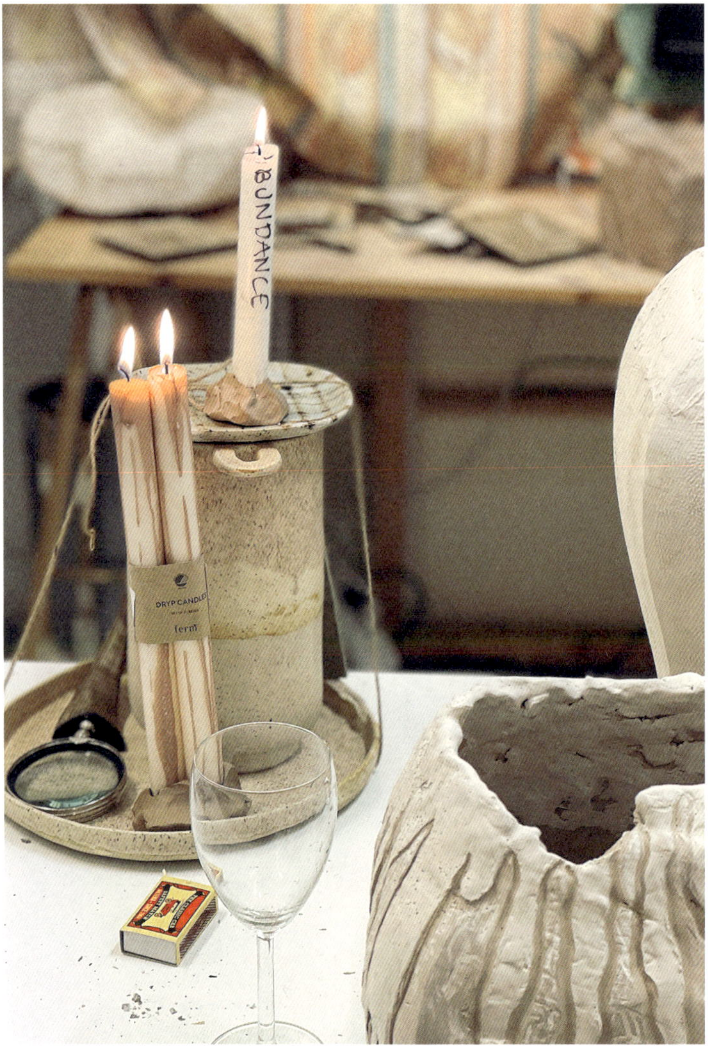
BUNDANCE
DRYP CANDLES
ferm

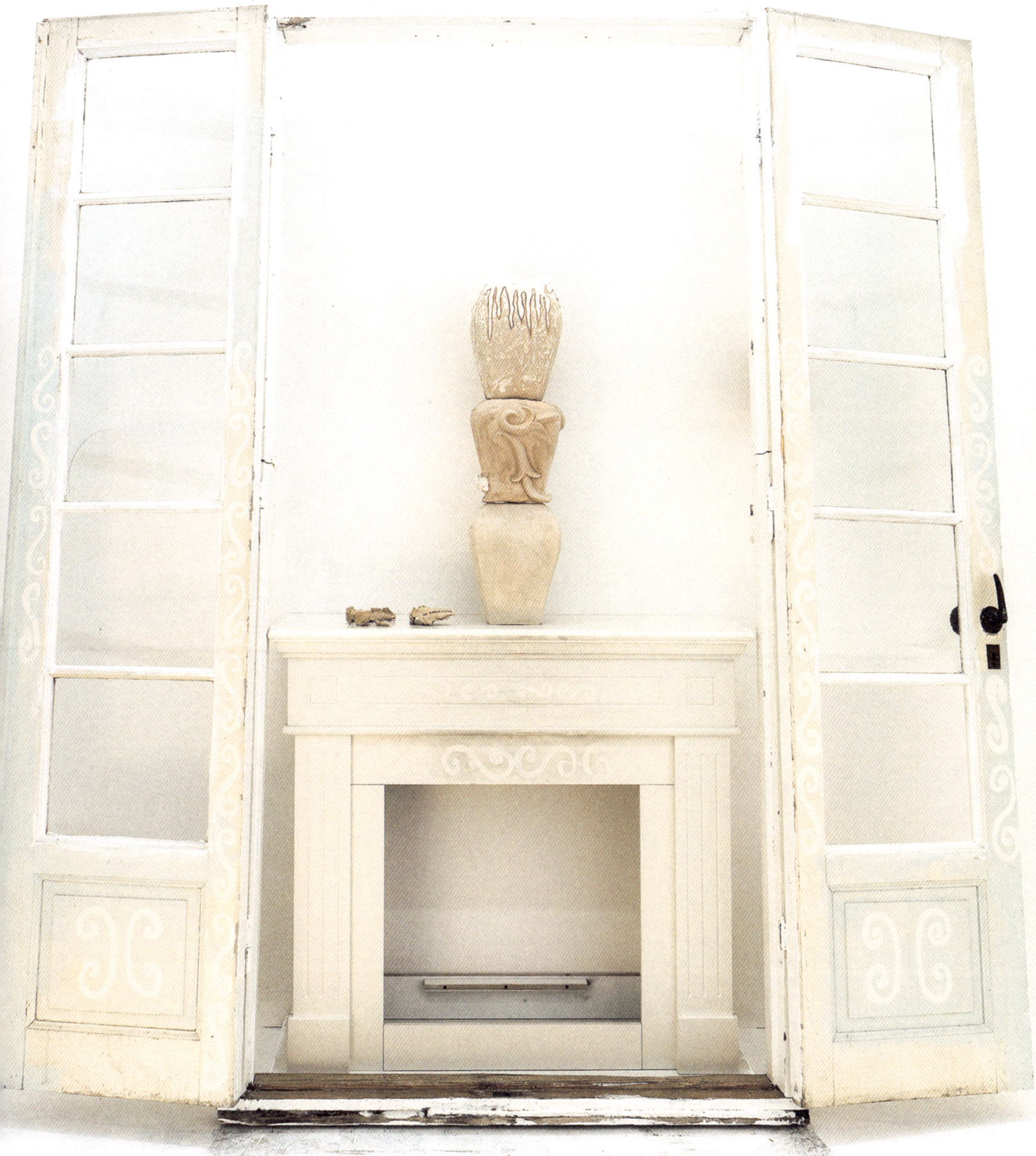

Jeanne Dunning

EXTRA SKIN (ADDING)
1999 · Video (11:30 min) · Acquired 1999

EXTRA SKIN (SUBTRACTING)
1999 · Video (9:57 min) · Acquired 1999

Where exactly is the self? Inside the body, or in relation to others? If one's own body is the starting point for getting to know and understanding the world, then Jeanne Dunning's practice can be said to explore the relationship between the body, the self, and society. The two video works *Extra Skin (Adding)* and *Extra Skin (Subtracting)* can be seen as two attempts to search for an understanding of the self, but also highlight the difficulty in getting there. In the first piece, we see a person putting on layer after layer of light skin-colored clothing. But rather than providing an increased sensitivity to the world, this new fleshy coating appears prosthetic, protective, and isolating. In the latter, a woman scrapes off layer after layer of skin and lets the scraped-off skin form a pile on the ground.

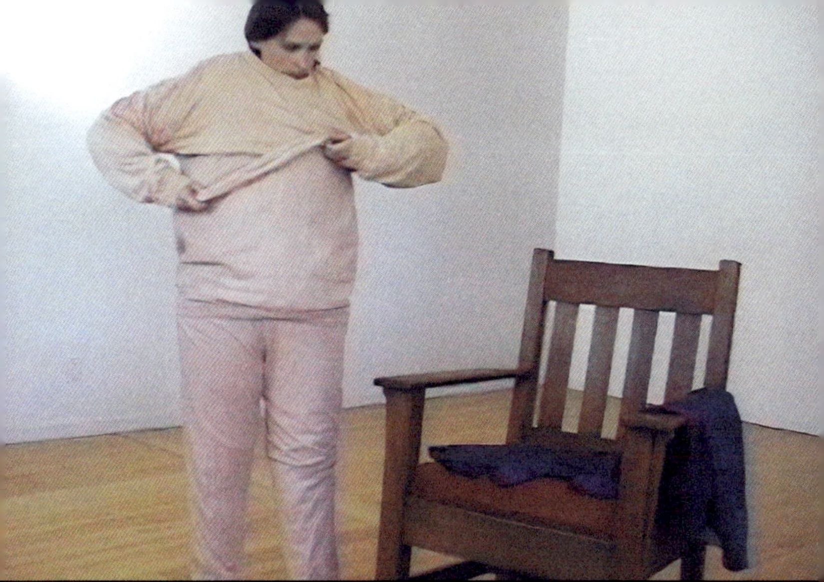

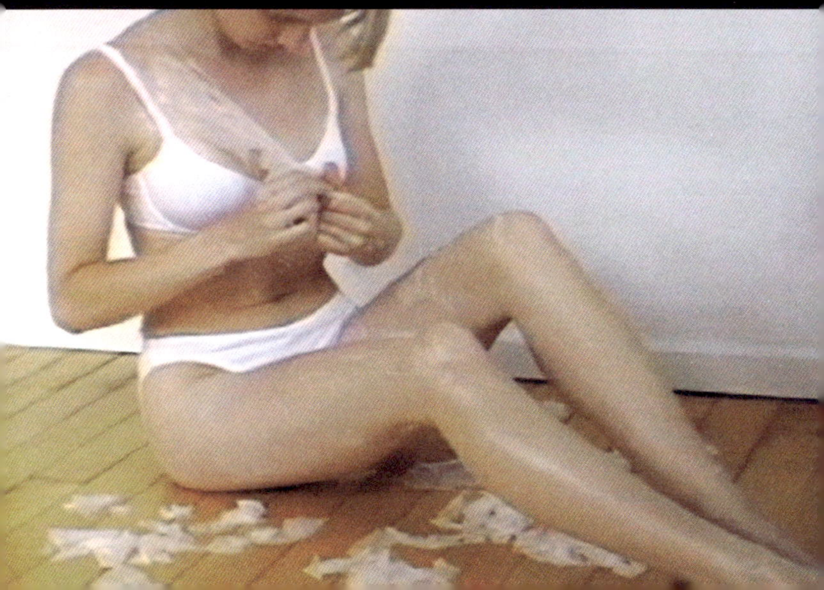

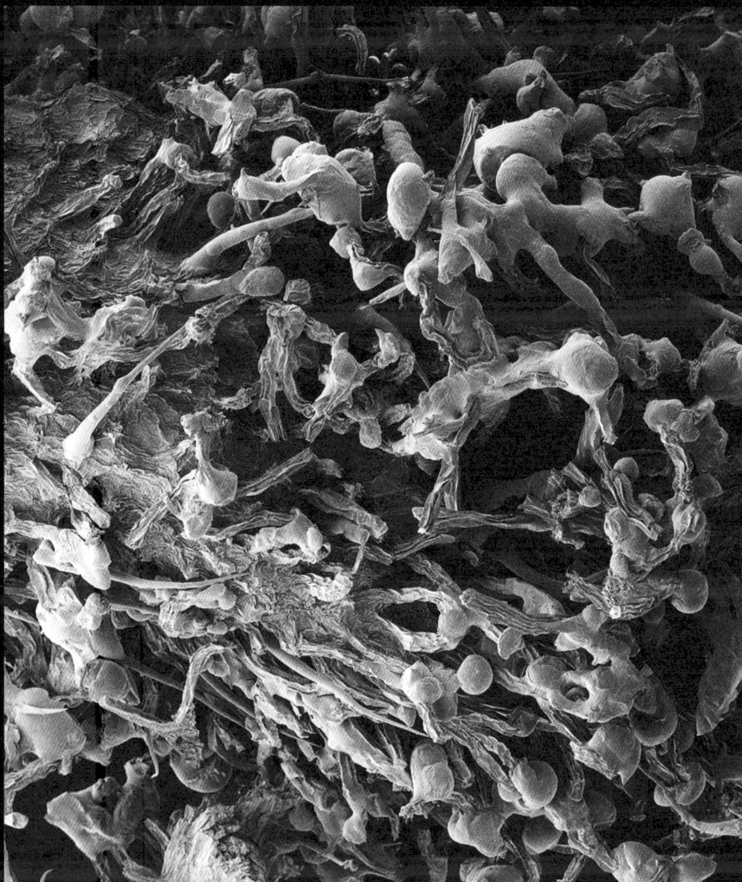

Joachim Koester

UNTITLED (CANNABIS #4)
2019 · Gelatin silver print · Acquired 2020

UNTITLED (COCAINE #8)
2019 · Gelatin silver print · Acquired 2020

'I think of these images as a kind of essence or condensation of the political and neurological effects of cocaine.' Joachim Koester's photographs *Untitled (Cannabis #4)* (p. 84) and *Untitled (Cocaine #8)* (pp. 86–87, detail) from the series *From the Secret Garden of Sleep* are taken with a scanning electron microscope that generates images by scanning objects with an electron beam with a raster pattern. In the series, he raises questions about how plants with narcotic effects can alter our consciousness and our experience of the world, but also points to their colonial history. For example, coca leaves have been used to control slaves and workers, as they reduce hunger and increase stamina. 'These images do not represent an abundance of happiness: rather, it is an abundance associated with the gates of Mordor or a free market economy,' Koester states.

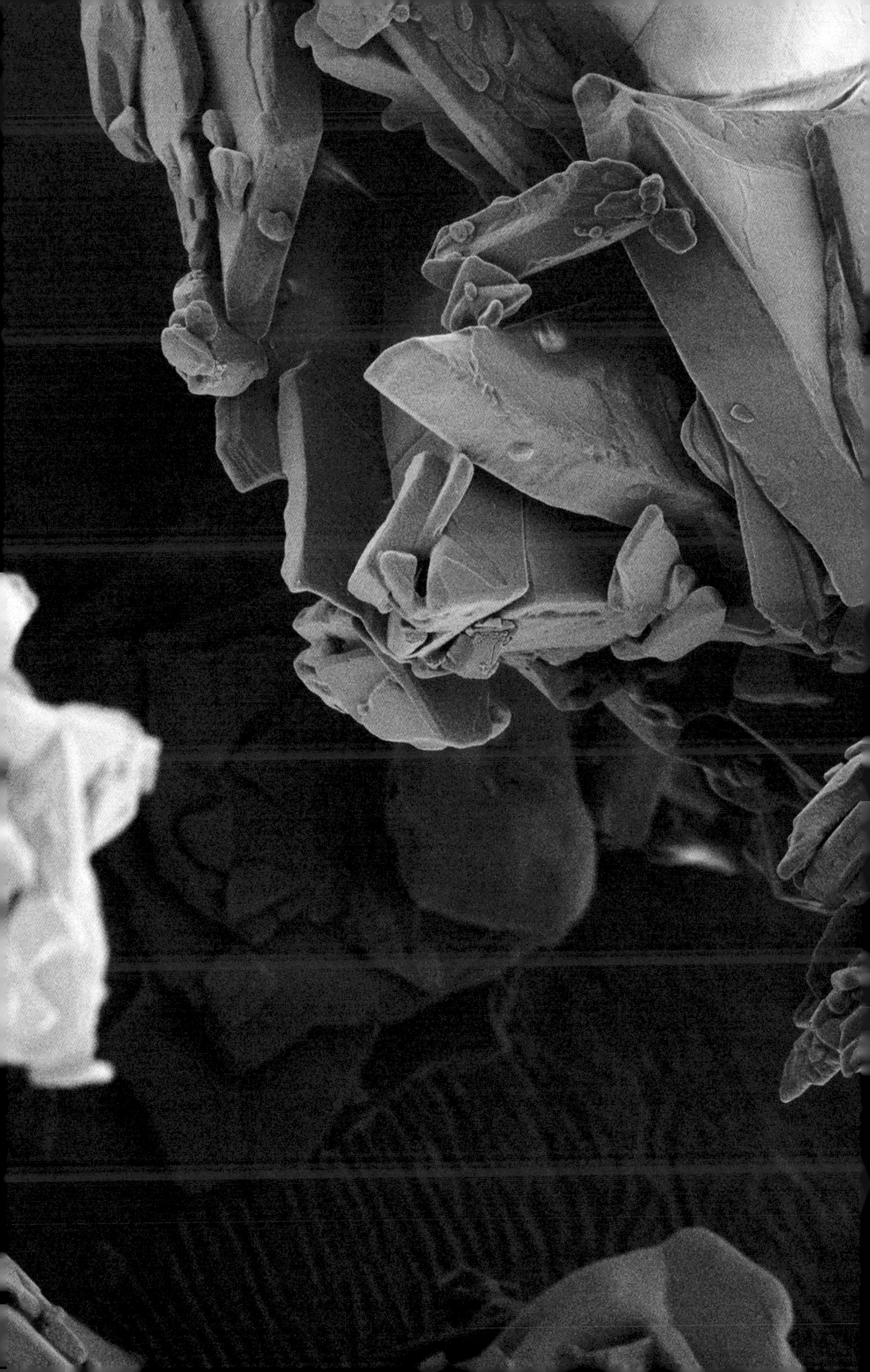

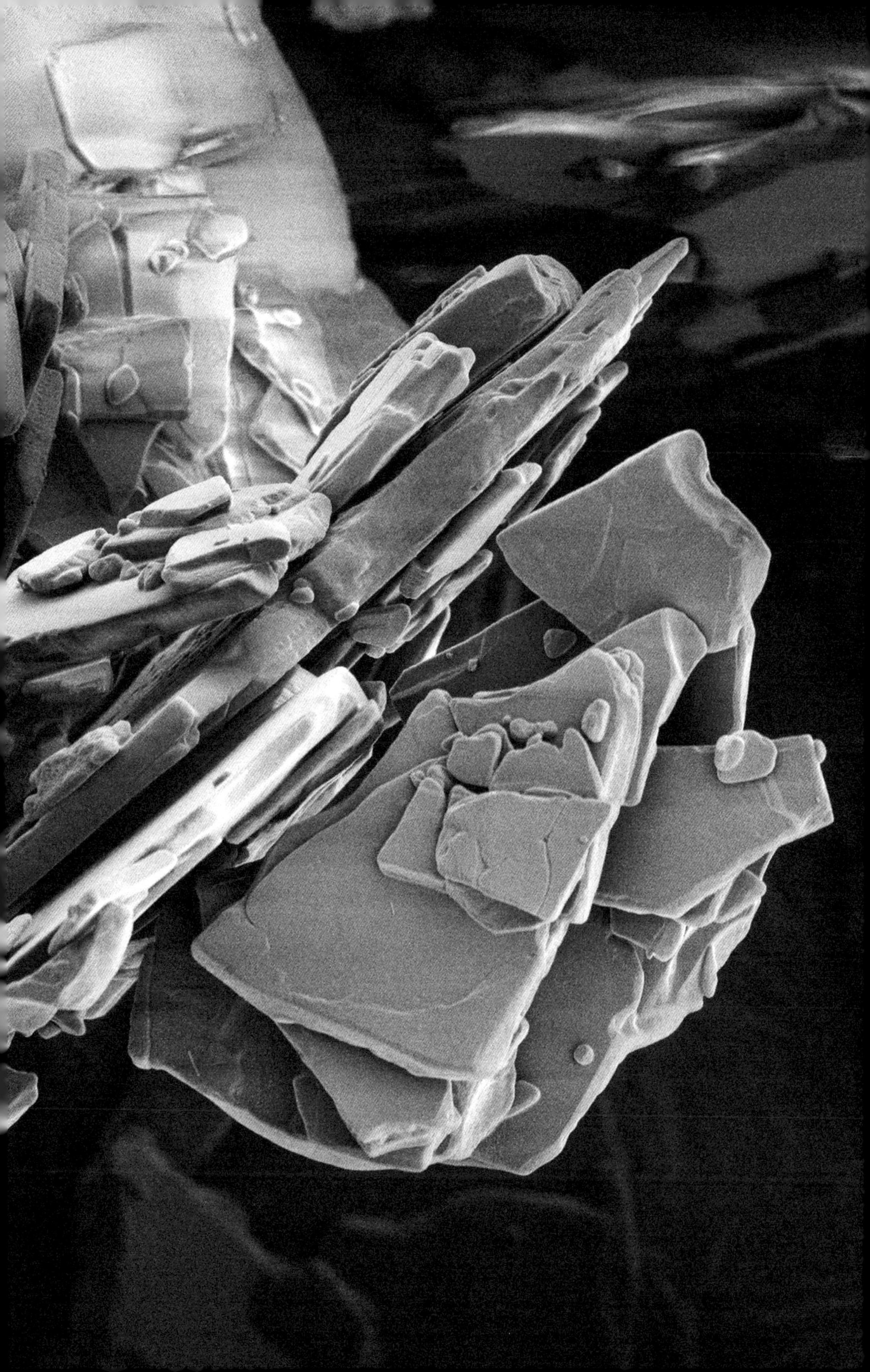

Iris Smeds

IN ORDER TO EAT ANOTHER MAN'S SOUL
2013 · Video (12:19 min) · Acquired 2023

DEATH YOGA
2015/24 · Performance lecture · Acquired 2023

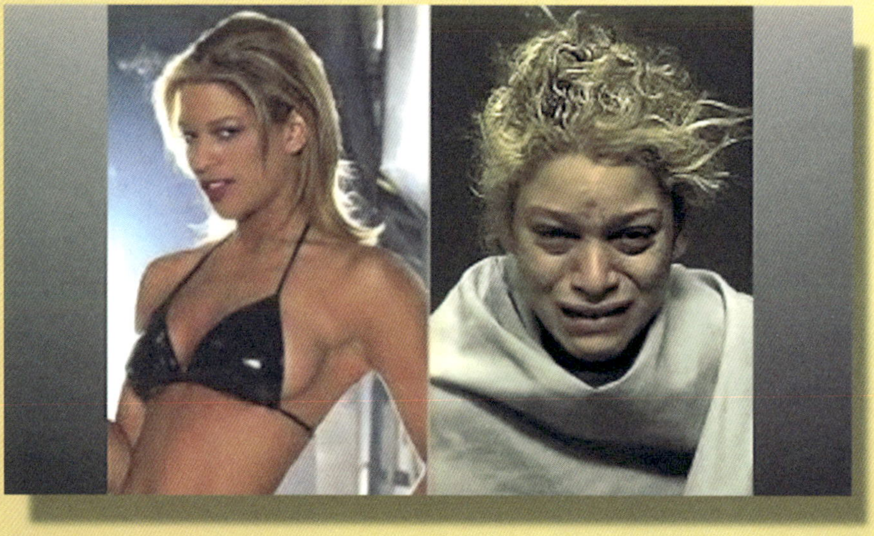

Iris Smeds' work revolves around narratives of success and marketability. In the video *In Order to Eat Another Man's Soul*, we see the artist in the role of a lecturer giving a presentation about the human soul. Through seductive affect, the lecturer contradicts the anti-aesthetic PowerPoint presentation's sincere message: the human soul is nothing more than a hole we fill with food, sex, drugs, and love in our pursuit of happiness. The solution, according to the lecturer, is to enter the art market, as works of art are the only objects that are animated by humans and at the same time can be purchased. Here, not only human desire is made visible, but also how the art market can be seen as a trade in souls. Taken to her extreme, she sees how capitalist society influences us to commodify our lives.

In the underachieving, nihilistic, and self-reinforcing performance lecture *Death Yoga*, death is seen as the ultimate act of resistance, when we are no longer inclined to produce and perform.

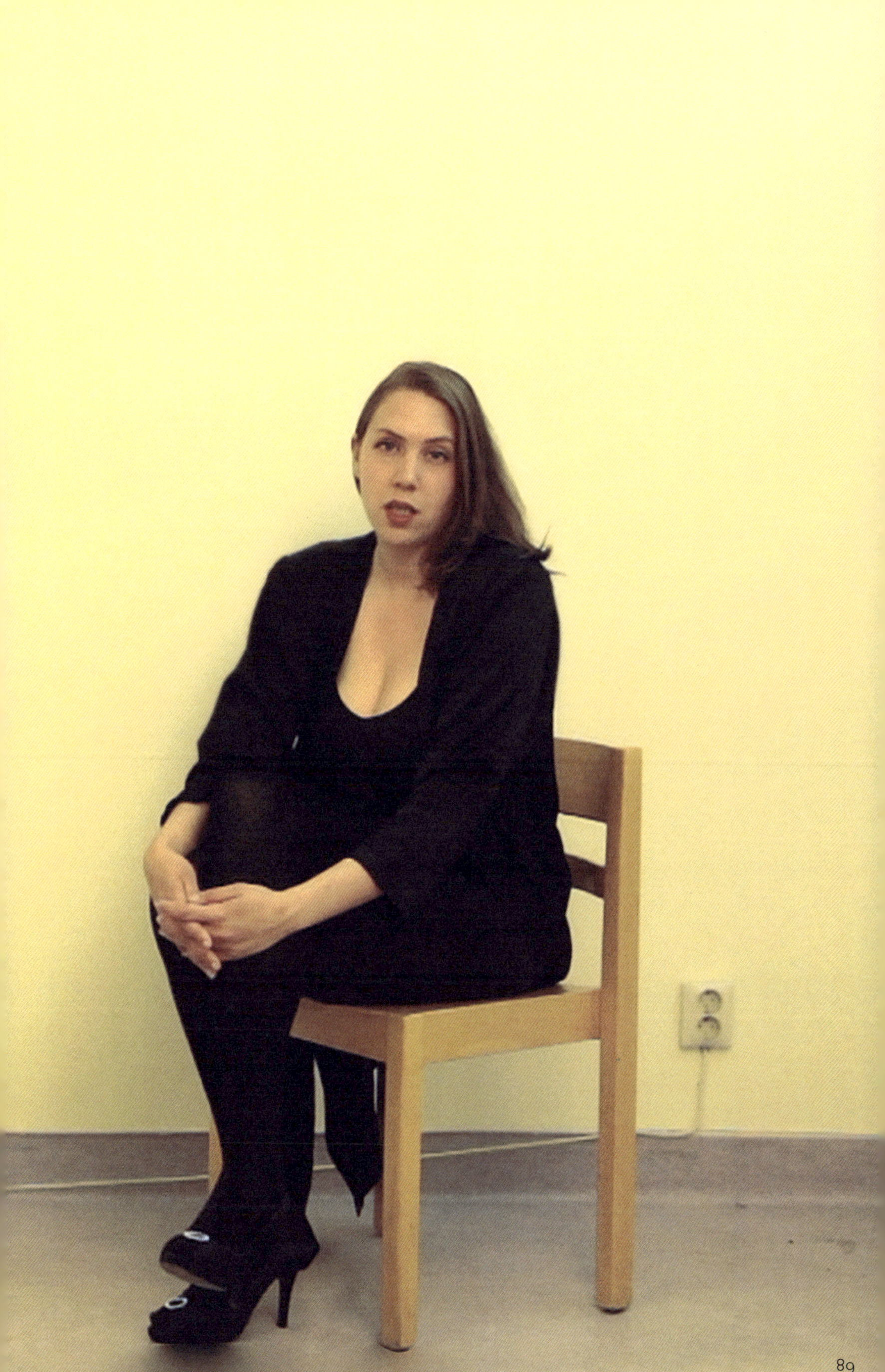

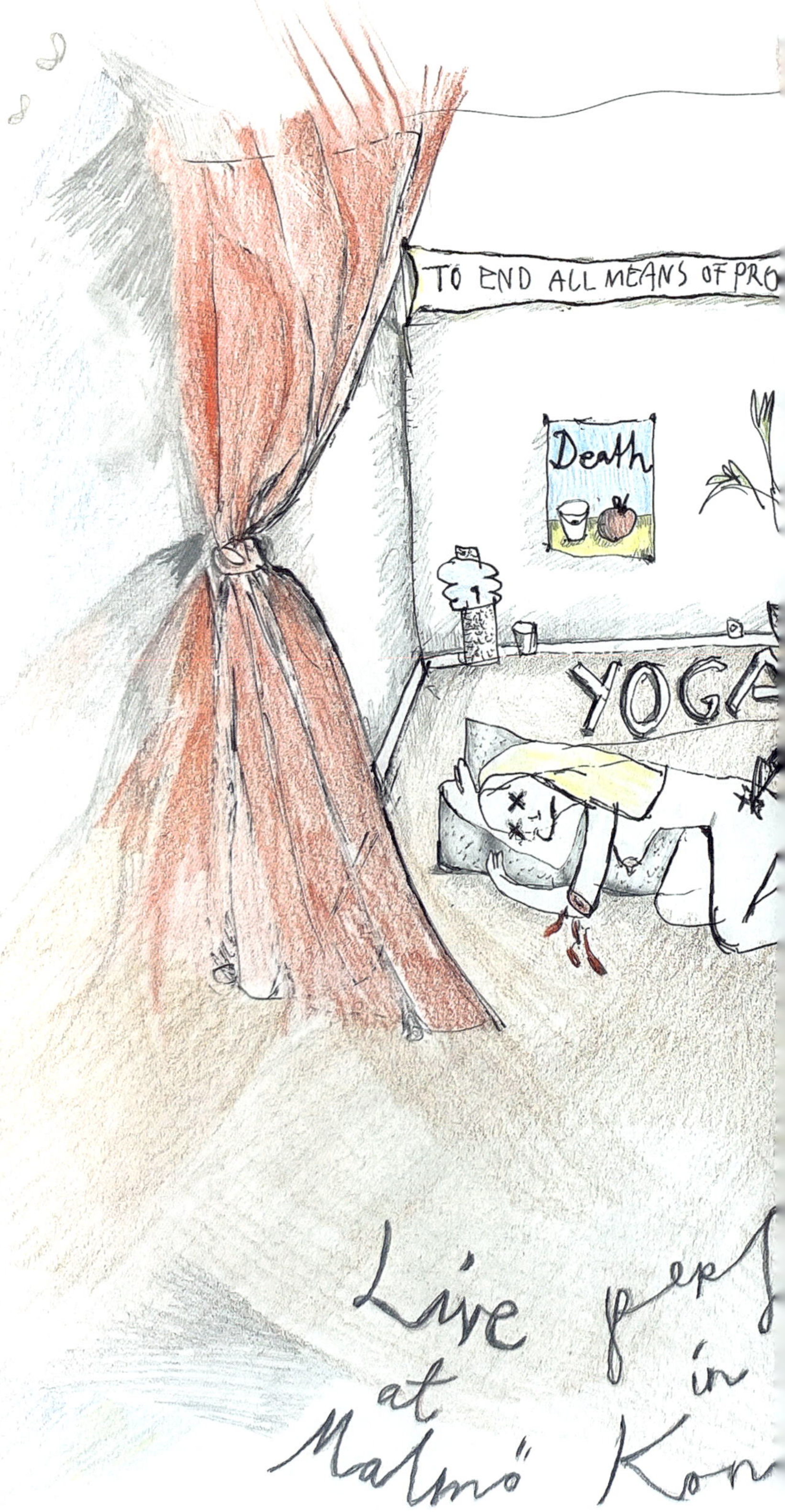
TO END ALL MEANS OF
Death
Live
at
in
Malmö

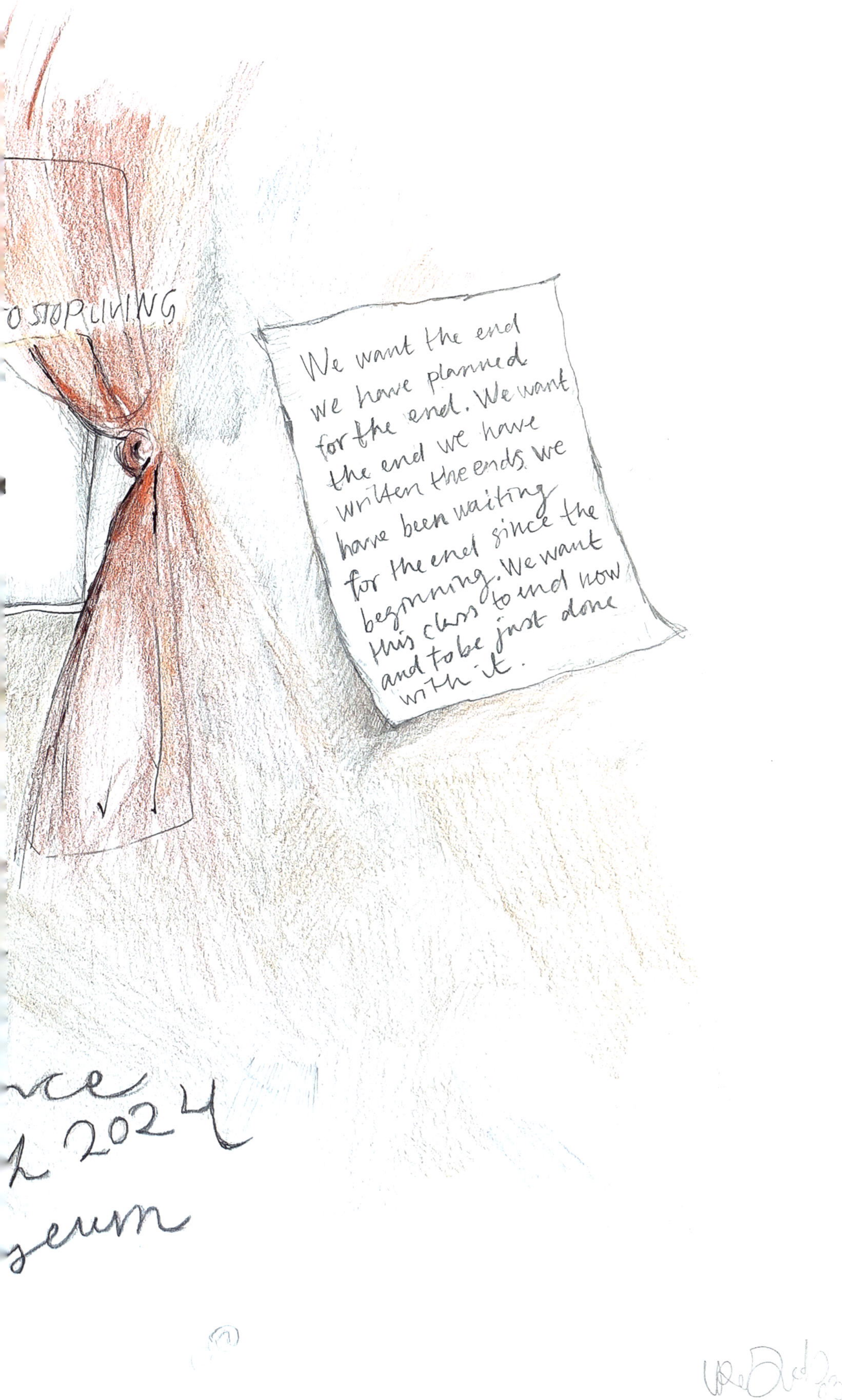
We want the end
we have planned
for the end. We want
the end we have
written the ends. We
have been waiting
for the end since the
beginning. We want
this class to end now
and to be just done
with it.

Gloria López Cleries

[ASMR] READING YOU TO SLEEP. SOFT-SPOKEN RELAXATION ABOUT AFFECTIVE CAPITALISM
2020 · Five videos (varying length) · In collaboration with Aino ASMR, Ailen Lucia ASMR, Abi ASMR, Easy ASMR and Articulate Design ASMR · Acquired 2023

Gloria López Cleries examines neoliberal rhetoric, emotional capitalism, and new forms of productivity, affect, and collectivity based on the tech industry and social media. In *[ASMR] Reading You to Sleep. Soft-Spoken Relaxation about Affective Capitalism*, she begins with symptoms that many suffer from, such as lack of sleep, anxiety and depression, and a viral trend which responds to these symptoms—ASMR (Autonomous Sensory Meridian Response). ASMR is a phenomenon where, for example, whispers and rustling induce shivers of pleasure in the listener. For the project, López Cleries has collaborated with five ASMR YouTubers who have published content where they present the artist's critical texts about the role of emotions in market economy. Among other things, the work illustrates how the need for alternative therapeutic and calming digital spaces is increasing, while also creating a subversive critical perspective from within.

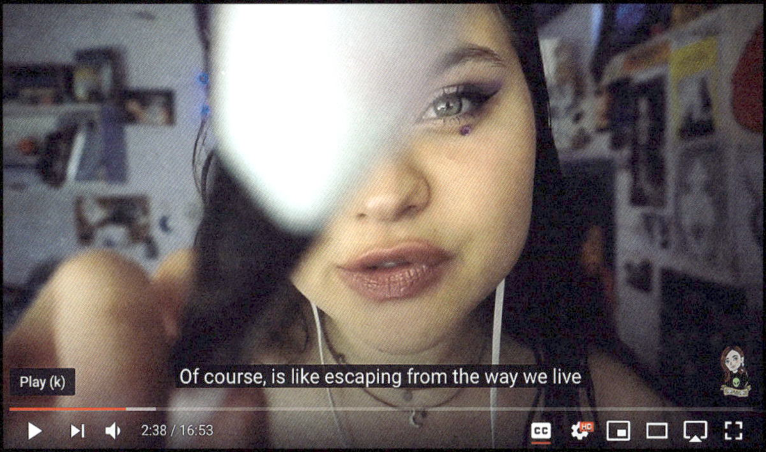
Play (k)
Of course, is like escaping from the way we live
2:38 / 16:53

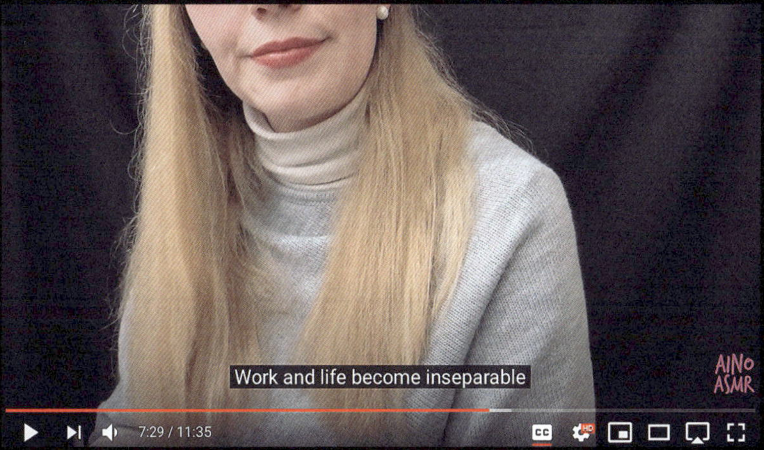
AINO
ASMR
Work and life become inseparable
7:29 / 11:35

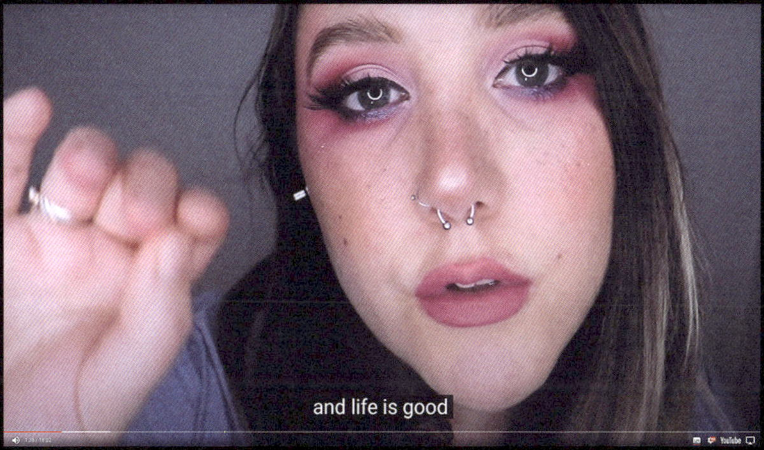
and life is good

Markus Copper

KNIVARE (KNIFER)

2008 · Sikaflex, sealant, iron, steel, machinery, sensor, electrical unit · Acquired 2008

When you approach the sculpture *Knivare* (Knifer), a motion sensor is activated, which in turn is connected to a long arm with a Mora knife—characteristic of the Mora region of Sweden—which slashes at you. Through his work, Markus Copper sought to address socio-political issues by activating emotions, such as fear, in the viewer. By actually experiencing emotions and not just reasoning about them, we may be able to understand both our own and others' actions. *Knivare* (Knifer) is a violent work that comments on human behavior and how human beings are often responsible for disasters. In his two previous large-scale works *Estonia* (2006) and *Kursk* (2004), Copper sought to tap into the collective fear caused by the sinking of both the passenger ferry Estonia and the nuclear submarine Kursk. He stated, 'I want my works to make people experience and feel something in this world.'

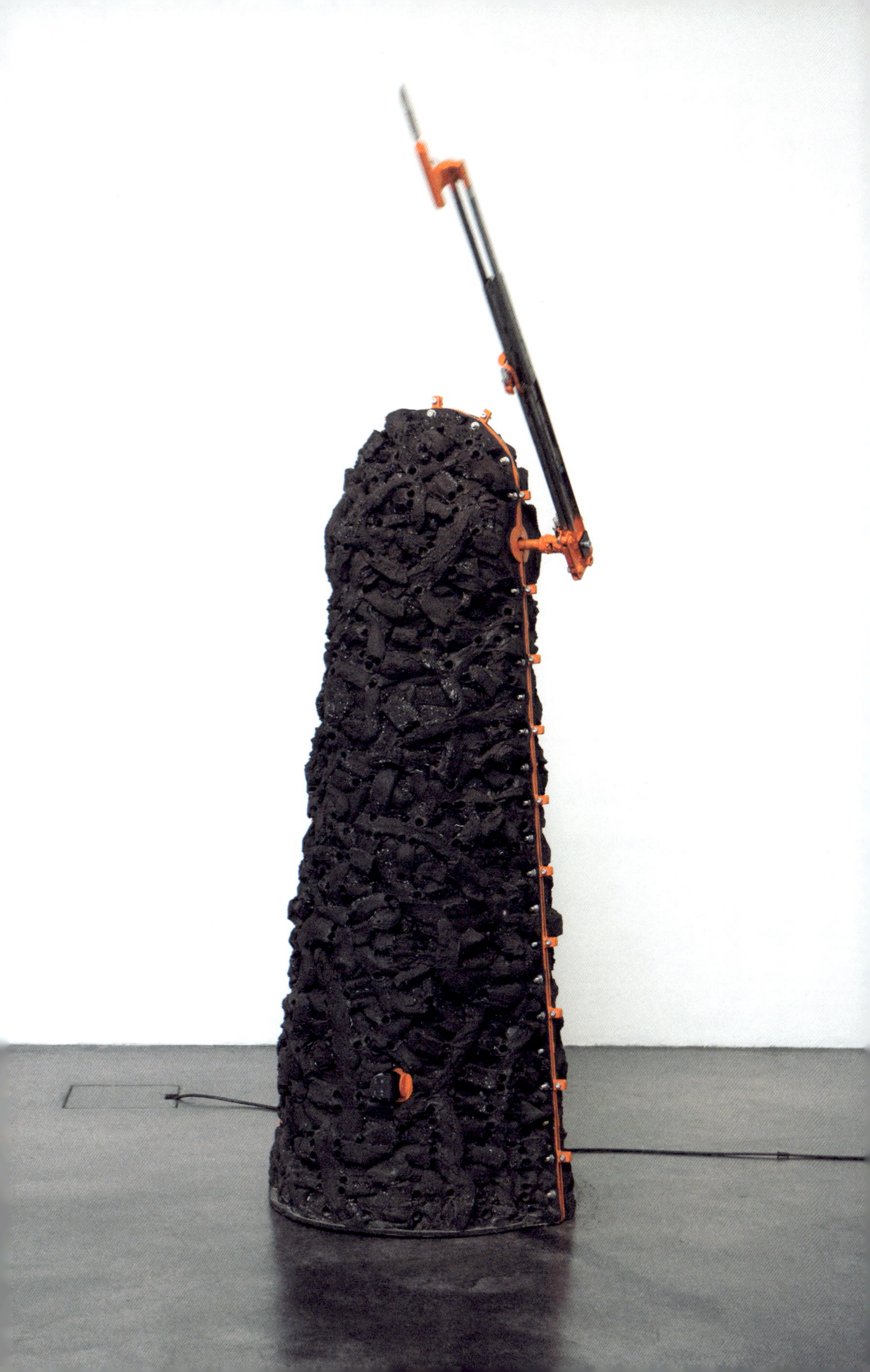

Muhammad Ali

FEARS FRESH
2009–11 · Prints · Acquired 2019

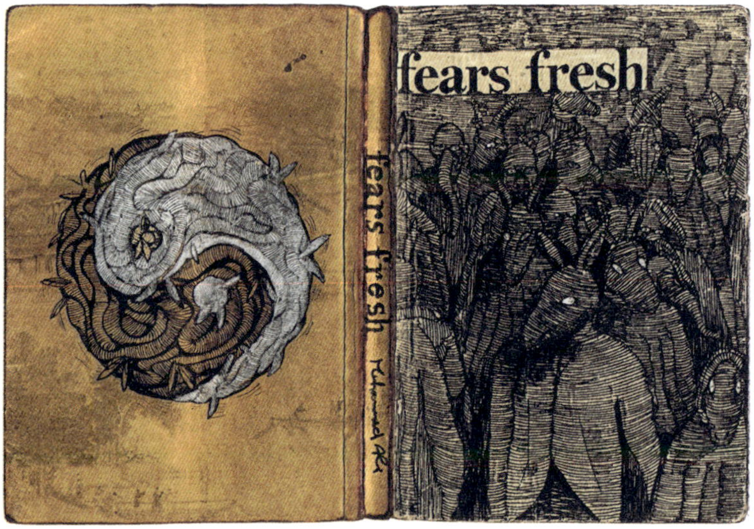

With *Fears Fresh*, an extensive series in the form of diary entries, Muhammad Ali has been working to depict the fear that something terrible is about to happen. The title comes from a piece in the *Financial Times*, where the words 'Fears Fresh'—new fears—appeared. In the series, Ali has transformed newspaper images and messages that he thought provided warning, as when animals seek shelter just before the storm. The drawings and collages can be seen as a way of dealing with personal anxiety before an impending war, but also give everyday fear a new face. The artist began to work on the series in 2009, two years before the Arab Spring erupted and the war in Syria broke out. He works in a variety of mediums with pieces that often touch on the space between consciousness and the subconscious, investigating how meaning is created and communicated.

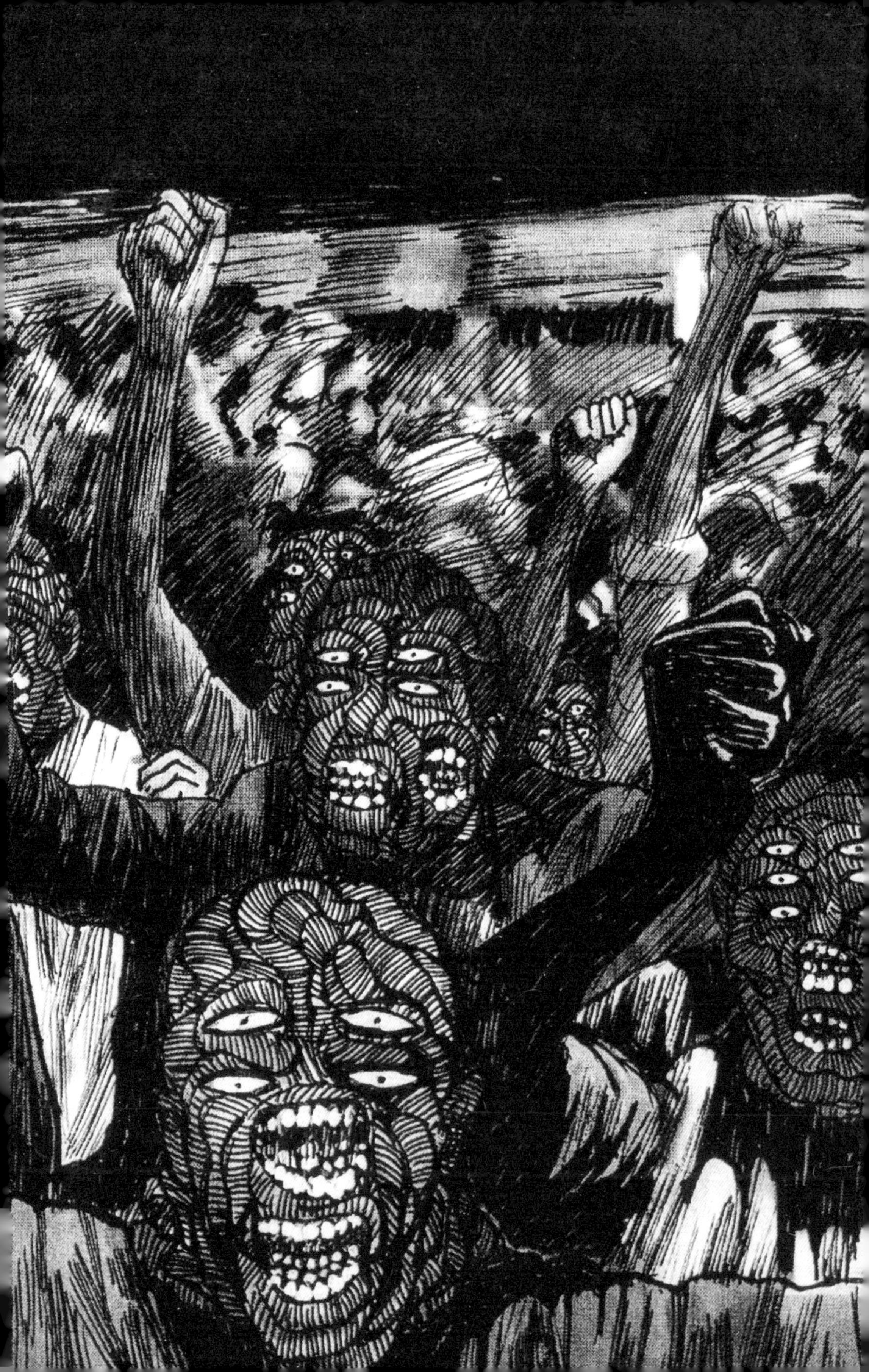

Muhammad Ali

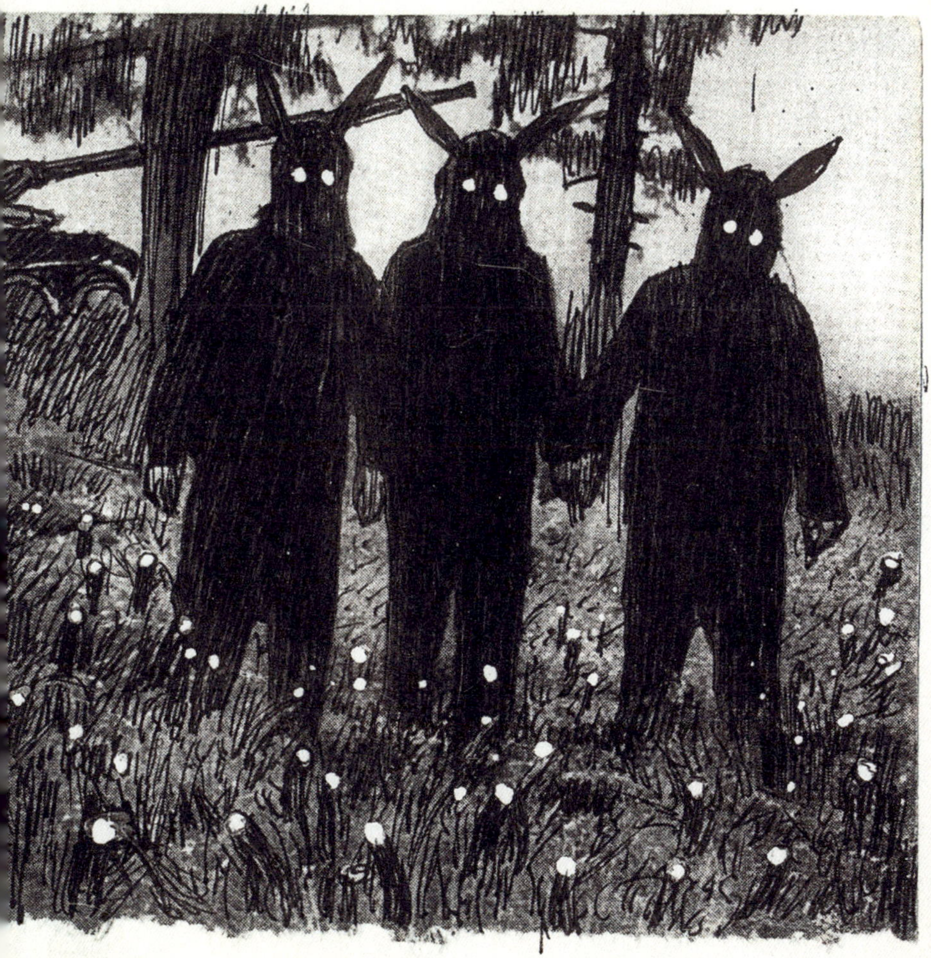

Truls Melin

UNTITLED
1998 · Wood, glass, iron · Acquired 2023

Four solid cupboards on legs stand on the floor. They all have different characteristics but are painted the same shade of pale pink, as if they were individuals forced into the same template. The monochrome whole is characteristic of Truls Melin's practice and recalls the serial system of minimalism. Unlike the minimalists, however, who aspired to strip away all forms of reference, his art was always anchored in personal memories and experiences. He talked about the works as 'sculptures of silence,' and working with them was a way for him to peel away the impressions from his surroundings.

Melin's work is characterized by a modesty that accommodates both playful and poetic expressions. The sculptural installation presented here invites ideas about the not always so easily reconciled need for authenticity in a culture that appears to be increasingly streamlined, and where both school and the workplace presuppose that you fit into the norm.

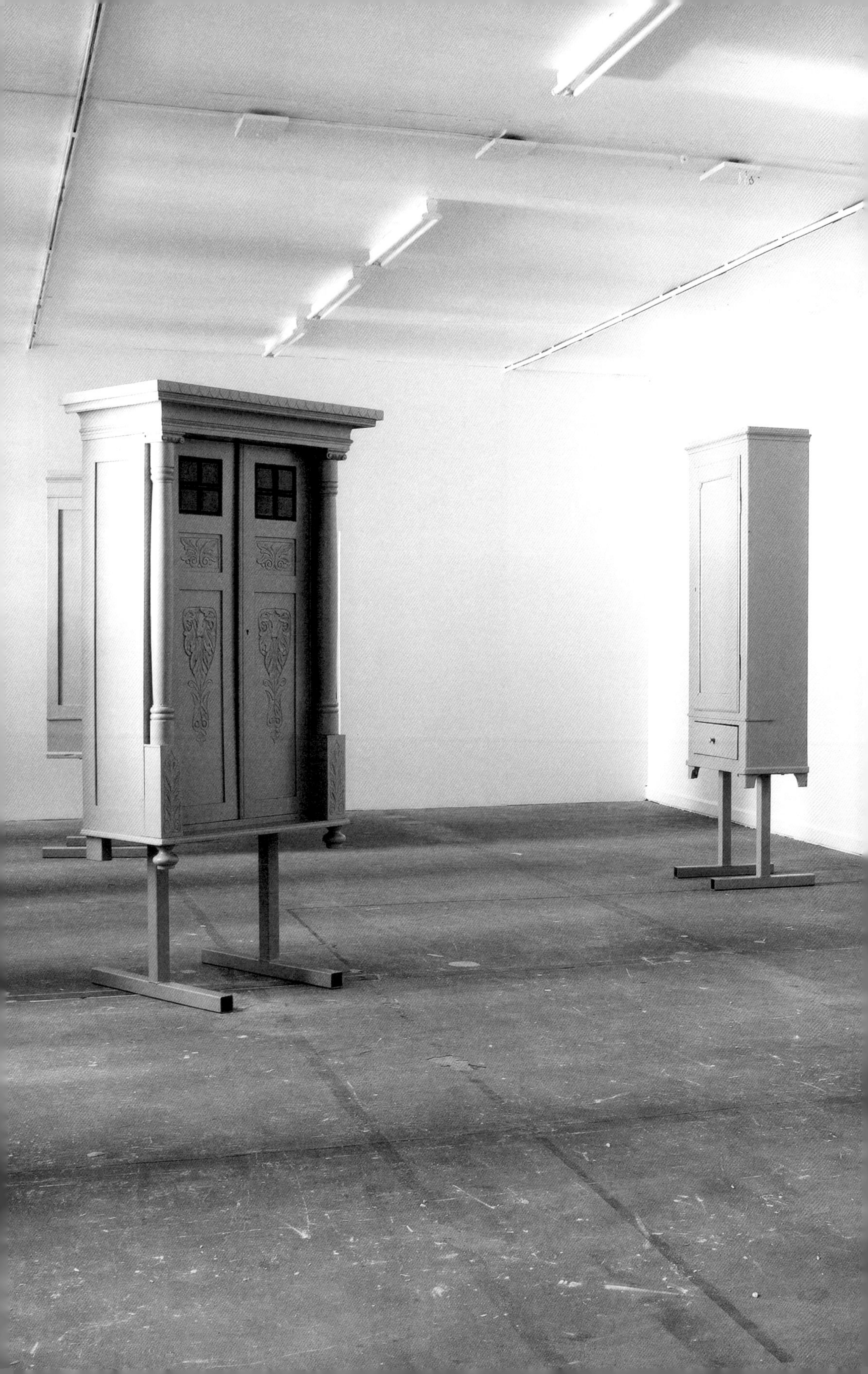

Elis Eriksson

VA DET ALLT (IS THAT IT)
2004 · Oil on canvas
Acquired 2004

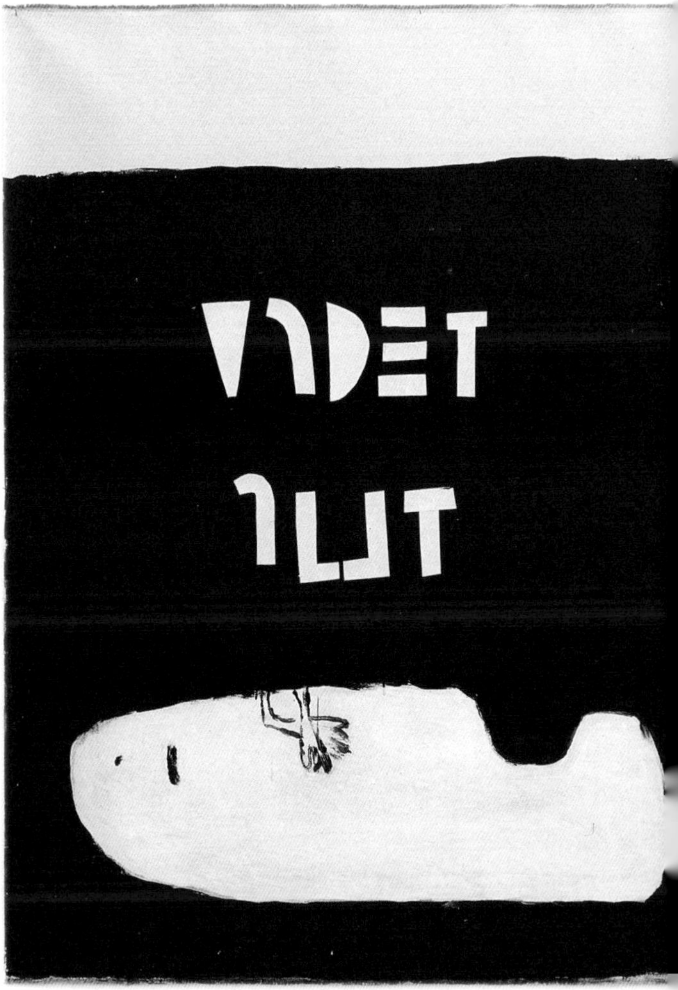

The nursing home is a crucial site for some of society's most vulnerable and fragile individuals. In the pursuit of greater returns, tax funds are simultaneously invested in care companies with anonymous owners and addresses in tax havens, while conditions for relatives and patients steadily get worse. Elis Eriksson addressed the capitalization on suffering and death from a care recipient's perspective in the 2004 exhibition *Låt lovsången ljuda, psaltaren 66:5–12* (Let the Song of Praise Ring, Book of Psalms 66:5–12) at Lars Bohman Gallery in Stockholm. Here, the painting *Va det allt* (Is That It) was included, which in large format depicts a set of individuals alongside text fragments such as 'we who are dying are a resource' (vi döende är en resurs) and 'and what a damn sad cold cut' (åkk vilket trist jävla pålägg) in Eriksson's characteristic manner. In an interview about his peculiar writing style, he said that the use of the phonetic and vernacular 'åkk' instead of the correctly spelled Swedish 'och' makes the reader pay attention and 'creates a void full of energy.' *Va det allt* (Is That It) was one of the final works in Eriksson's extensive socially engaged practice, which often revolved around lifting the voice of the little person.

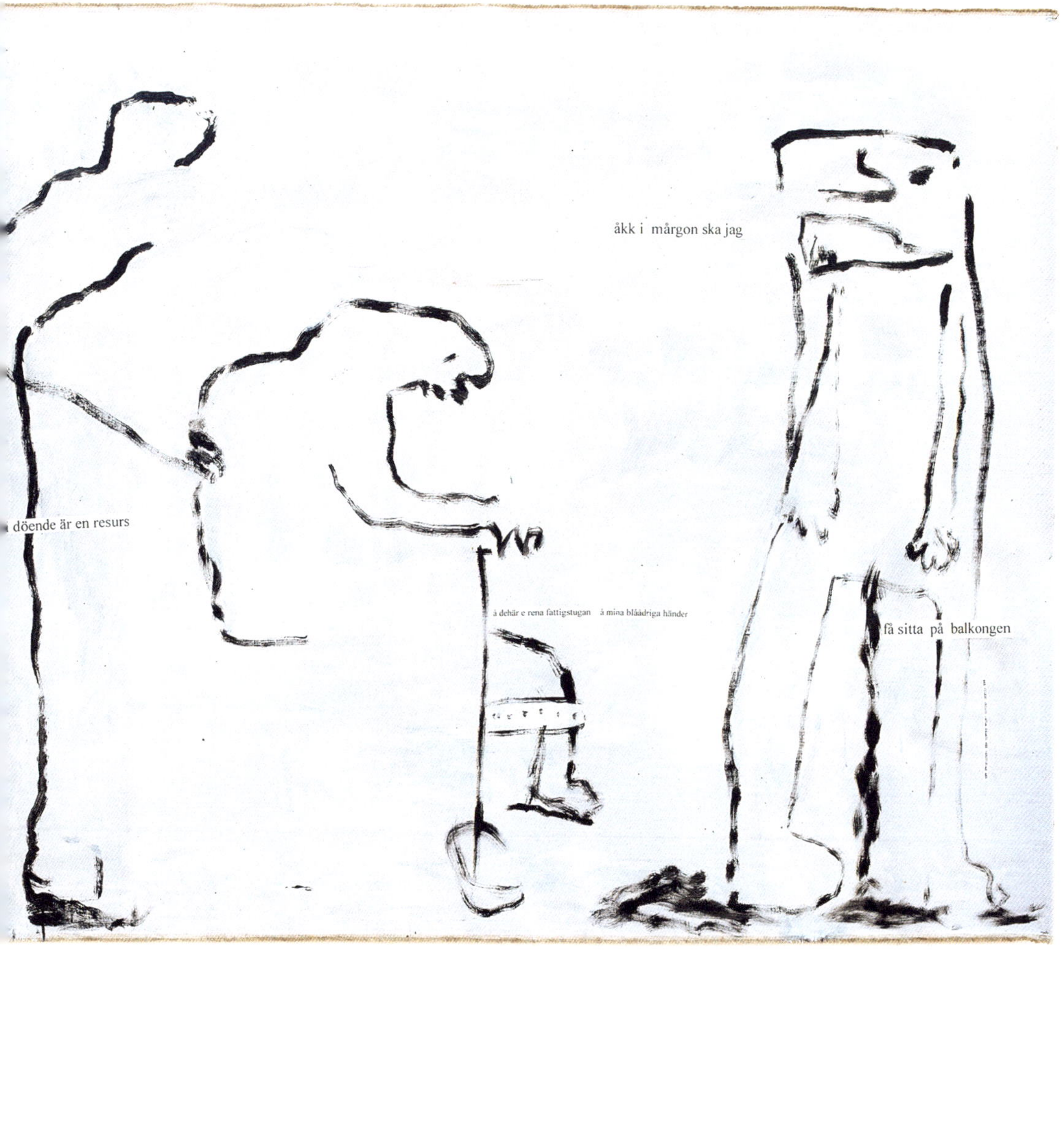
åkk i mårgon ska jag
döende är en resurs
å dehär e rena fattigstugan å mina blåådriga händer
få sitta på balkongen

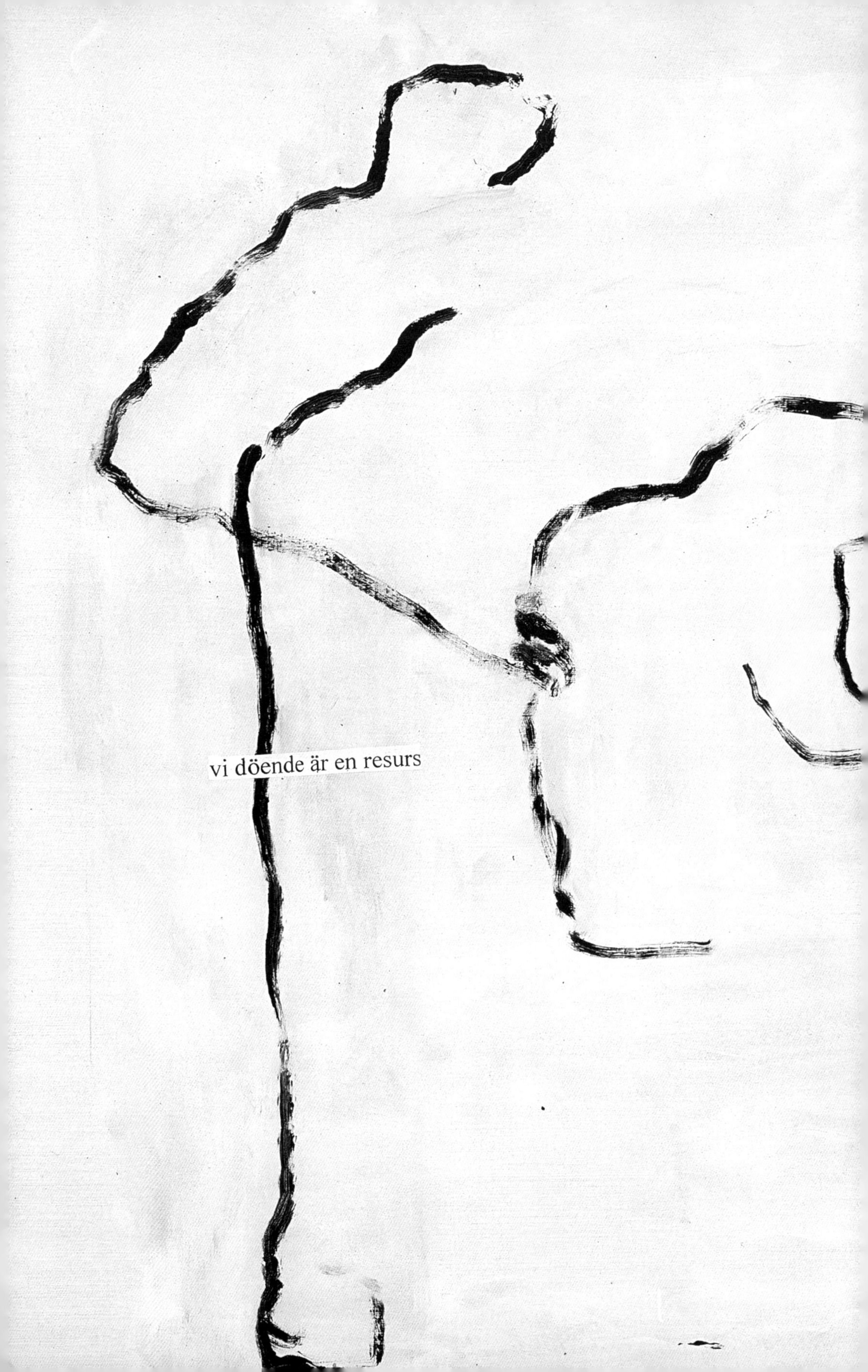
vi döende är en resurs

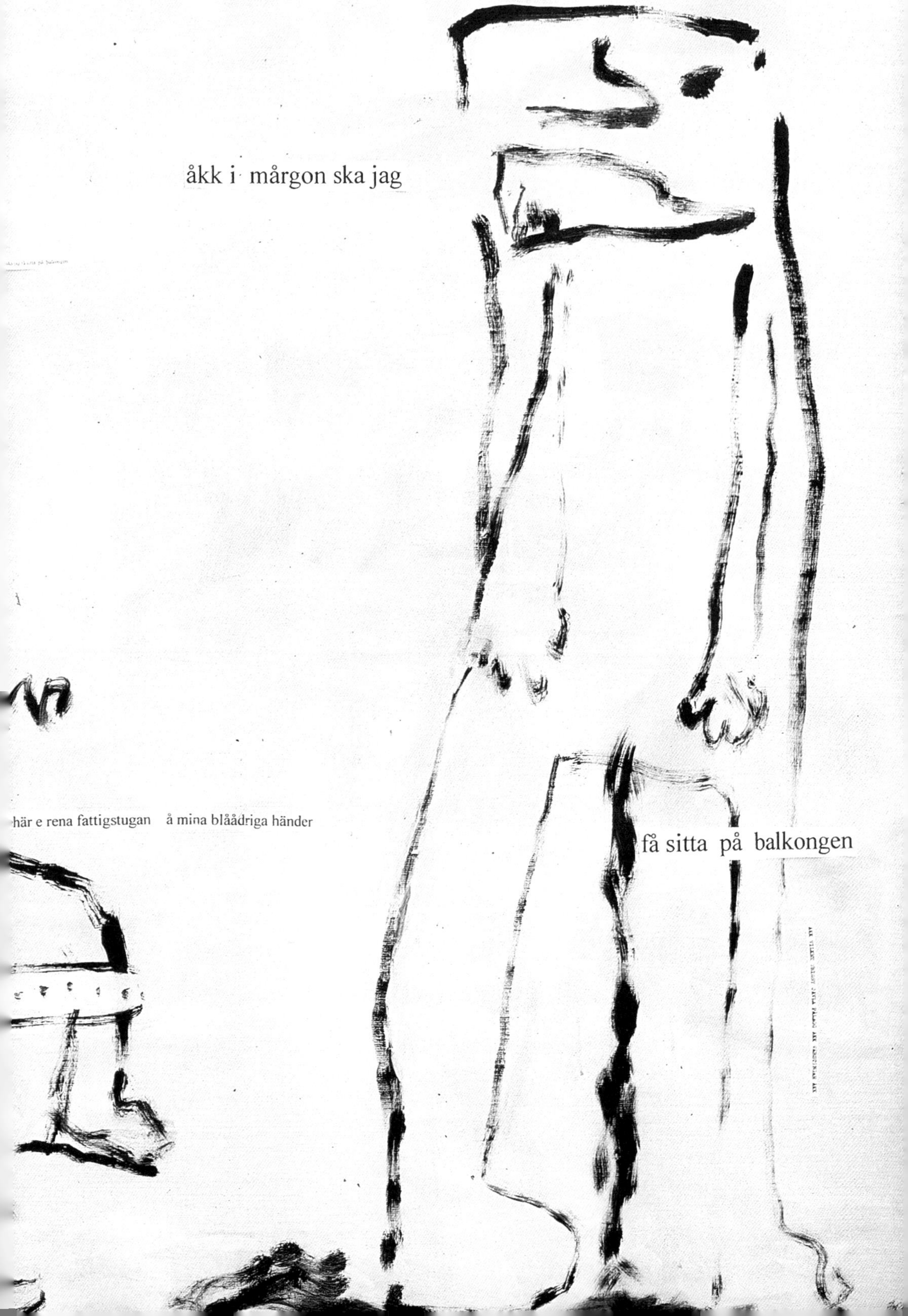

åkk i mårgon ska jag
här e rena fattigstugan
å mina blåådriga händer
få sitta på balkongen

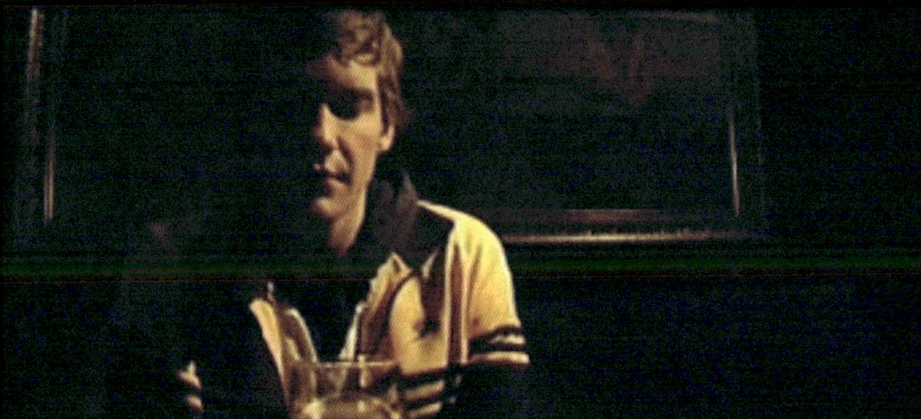

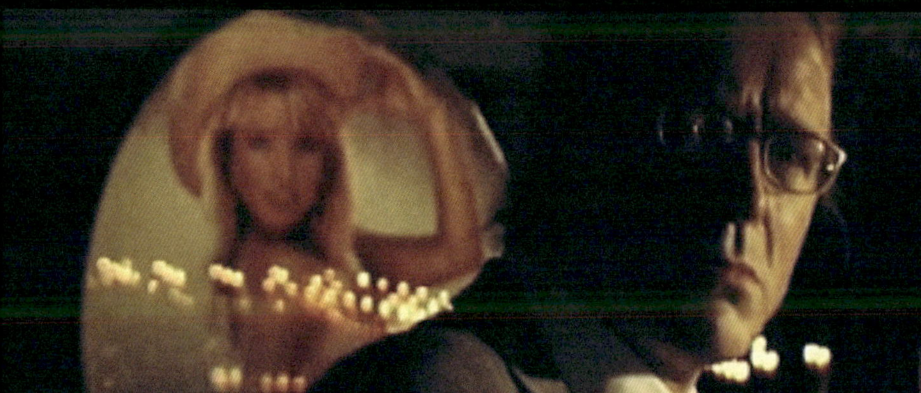

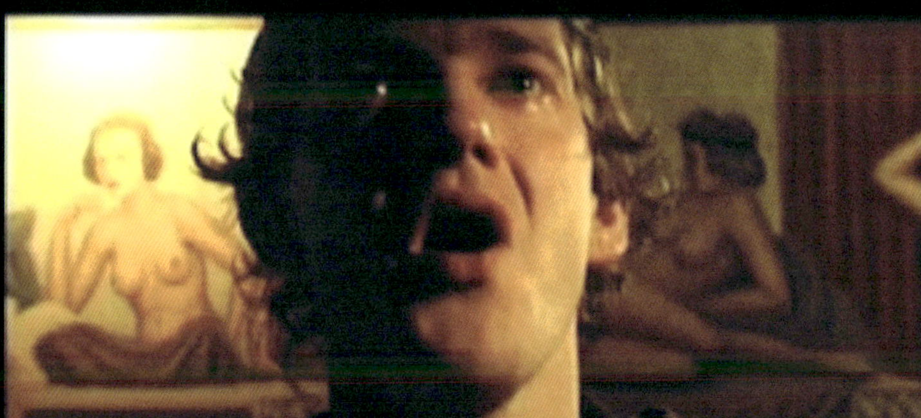

Jesper Just

NO MAN IS AN ISLAND II
2004 · Video (4 min) · Acquired 2004

In Jesper Just's video work *No Man Is an Island II*, five men of varying ages sit alone, each with a beer, in a strip club where the atmosphere can be described as melancholy and dejected. The mood becomes both comical and touching as the youngest man bursts into Roy Orbison's forlorn ballad *Crying*, and the others join in one after the other. The piece highlights how social conventions are tied to place and gender as well as which feelings and desires can be shared. *No Man Is an Island II* is part of the trilogy *A Fine Romance* (2002–4), which deals with norms regarding masculinity, community, vulnerability, and social expectations. The works explore notions concerning agency, performativity, and interpassivity, a concept formulated in the 1990s by Robert Pfaller and Slavoj Žižek. Just proposes that he in his work mobilizes interpassivity by delegating feelings and moods to make other people feel what you feel.

Biographies

Muhammad Ali (b. 1982, Syria) works in drawing, video, and installation, where he investigates how meaning is constructed and understood. Ali has exhibited at several institutions, including Moderna Museet (Stockholm), AllArtNow Syria (Damascus), Bornholms Kunstmuseum, and Pori Art Museum, and has had residencies at, among others, Botkyrka konsthall, Delfina Foundation (London), and IASPIS (Stockholm). He is educated at Konstfack—University of Arts, Crafts and Design (Stockholm) and Damascus University.

Andréason & Leibel (Kristian Andréason, b. 1974; Kristin Leibel, b. 1972, Sweden) is a multidisciplinary design studio in Malmö, and the graphic designers for *Happily Ever After*. Educated at HDK-Valand, University of Gothenburg, their innovative and exploratory design work has been exhibited in various international design hubs, including Milan, London, Eindhoven, Paris, and Tokyo.

Nina Björk (b. 1967, Sweden) is an author and critic based in Lund. She made her debut in 1996 with the book *Under det rosa täcket: om kvinnlighetens vara och feministiska strategier* (Under the Pink Cover: On the Being of Femininity and Feminist Strategies). Her most recent book is *Om man älskar frihet: tankar kring det politiska* (If You Love Freedom: Thoughts on the Political [2020]).

Julia Björnberg (b. 1983, Sweden) is curator of the exhibition *Happily Ever After* and has served as curator at Malmö Konstmuseum since 2022. Previously curated and co-curated exhibitions include *Signe Johannessen—Trophy* (Ystads konstmuseum, 2021–22), *Hannah Ryggen—Weaving the World* (Moderna Museet Malmö, 2015–16), and *Heed the Call—Art for All!* (Malmö Konstmuseum, 2016). She is also one of the initiators of *Den platta jorden*, an international network for artistic exploration of the local.

Anita Christoffersson (b. 1943, Sweden) works with non-figurative images in disparate materials and by linking preexisting textiles, objects, and words. Her work often addresses existential themes connected to the human, the personal, and the private. She is educated at Goldsmiths, University of London, and has previously exhibited in Australia, Denmark, England, Finland, Japan, and Sweden.

Markus Copper (1968–2019, Finland) worked primarily with large-scale spatial works that utilize sound, mechanical movement, and light. Much of his work comments on human action, morals, and mental landscapes. He graduated from the Academy of Fine Arts, Helsinki, in 1995 and received the Ars Fennica Award in 1999.

Jeanne Dunning (b. 1960, USA) explores our relationship with our physicality, the strange and unfamiliar in the body, gender, and notions of normality and death through photography, sculpture, and video. Since the late 1980s, her work has been exhibited internationally, including at the Whitney Biennial (New York), the Sydney Biennial, and the Venice Biennale.

Stina Ebers (b. 1962, Sweden) primarily works with sculptures and installations that are constructed from non-traditional materials such as peat, asphalt, waste oil, and nail polish. Her work is deeply rooted in contemporary existential issues and has been exhibited at institutions including Moderna Museet Malmö, Millesgården (Stockholm), and Ystads konstmuseum.

Elis Eriksson (1906–2006, Sweden) worked as a traditional sculptor after completing his education at the Royal Swedish Academy of Fine Arts in Stockholm. His artistic practice subsequently developed in the direction of a Dadaist stance and, starting in the early 1960s, his work also featured conceptual strains. Around then, he began documenting his daily life and meetings with people and collected a range of everyday traces of these encounters.

Helena Fernández-Cavada (b. 1979, Spain) explores questions of existential health and well-being through participant-based performances, drawing, sound, publications, and video. She is educated at the Facultad de Bellas Artes, Universidad Complutense de Madrid, and has exhibited at, among others, Marabouparken konsthall (Stockholm), Krognoshuset (Lund), Matadero Madrid, and Arróniz Arte Contemporáneo (Mexico City).

Ester Fleckner (b. 1983, Denmark) is an artist whose practice addresses queer and trans perspectives materialized in series of woodcuts, drawings, texts, and concrete installations. By drawing upon abstraction, Fleckner destabilizes established categories of gender, body, and sexuality and opens up for new forms of representation. Educated at the Royal Danish Academy of Fine Arts in Copenhagen and Goldsmiths, University of London.

Jenny Grönvall (b. 1973, Finland) is a performance artist based in Malmö and educated at Malmö Art Academy and Konstfack—University of Arts, Crafts and Design (Stockholm). Grönvall works with spatial and social installations addressing issues regarding room for action, aesthetics, and power. Her work has been exhibited at Dunker's Cultural Center (Helsingborg), Göteborg International Biennial for Contemporary Art, Moderna Museet Malmö, Kunsthall Oslo, Silvershed (New York), and Malmö Konsthall, among others.

Ramón Guillén-Balmes (1954–2001, Spain) worked with sculpture in a range of different materials. He studied at La Llotja in Barcelona where he became part of the Experimental Workshop of Plastic Arts (TEAP). In his projects, he often took as his point of departure human needs and desires, automatism, and human anatomy. He was deeply influenced by Dadaism and also used *objets trouvés* to decontextualize everyday objects. His work has been exhibited at, among others, Bo01 (Malmö), CIRCA (Montreal), and MACBA (Barcelona).

Sive Hamilton Helle (b. 1989, Norway) is a filmmaker, visual artist, and lecturer based in Oslo. In her work, she explores the connection between humans and the environment through a critical examination of current debates regarding history, technology, and industry. She has an MFA in film from HDK-Valand, University of Gothenburg, and a BA from the London College of Communication.

Leif Holmstrand (b. 1972, Sweden) is a writer, musician, and artist who assumes an anti-straight historiography when they attack the world and memories in textile assemblage sculptures, long and absurd performance pieces, drawings, novels, composite images, text-sound compositions, poems, and erroneous pop songs. Their most recently published books are the novel *Kartritartornet* (The Cartographer's Tower [2023]) and the poetry collection *Inte världen* (Not the World [2022]). Their most recent major exhibition was the retrospective *From the Depth* at Marabouparken konsthall (2021–22).

Adelita Husni-Bey (b. 1985, Italy) is an artist and researcher. Through drawing, painting, video, and participant-based workshops, she focuses on micro-utopias, collective memories, and on interrogating the mechanisms behind political and economic power and control. Her work is recognized internationally and she has exhibited at the Venice Biennale, the Gwangju Biennale, BAK (Utrecht), MoMA (New York), and Museo Reina Sofía (Madrid).

E.B. Itso (b. 1977, Denmark) works, under one of his aliases, mainly with analogue photography, 16mm film, constructions and installations, as well as public works. Themes in his artwork are often neglected and overlooked places, underground phenomena, vulnerable people in the periphery or on the wrong side of the law. E.B. Itso is educated at Malmö Art Academy.

Anna Johansson (b. 1976, Sweden) is curator at Malmö Konstmuseum and curator of *Happily Ever After*. In recent years, she has curated and co-curated several group exhibitions at the museum, including *Shapeshifters* (2020), *Oomph: The Women Who Made Sweden Colorful* (2017), and *Heed the Call—Art for All!* (2016). She is also one of the initiators of *Den platta jorden*, an international network for artistic exploration of the local.

Kirse Junge-Stevnsborg (b. 1974, Denmark) has served as director of Malmö Konstmuseum since 2019. Previously, she worked as project manager at ART 2030. From 2009 to 2018, she was artistic director of Den Frie Centre of Contemporary Art in Copenhagen, and from 2006 to 2009, she worked as director of Gävle Art Center. She serves on multiple boards, including SMK—National Gallery of Denmark, CHART Art Fair, ADBC, and the Faculty of Fine and Performing Arts at Lund University.

Jesper Just (b. 1974, Denmark) works with video concerning questions of visual language and representation; how we create images and how these images contribute to our understanding of bodies, expectations, identities, social conventions, and how our self-esteem is subsequently affected. His extensive output has been exhibited around the world, including at the Venice Biennale, Palais de Tokyo (Paris), ARoS (Aarhus), and Performa (New York).

Joachim Koester (b. 1962, Denmark) works with photography and film, often in the borderland between the documentary and the fictive. His work has been exhibited at serval biennials, such as documenta X (1997), the Busan Biennale (2006), Manifesta 7 (2008), the 54th Venice Biennale (2011), and the Taipei Biennale (2012). His work is represented in various museum collections including MoMA (New York), Centre Pompidou (Paris), S.M.A.K. (Ghent), and Museo Reina Sofía (Madrid).

Jukka Korkeila (b. 1968, Finland) works with paintings that revolve around the male body, its vulnerability and sensuality. The works have serious undertones but are often portrayed with a clear sense of humor. He has studied architecture, design, and art in Helsinki, and his work has been exhibited around the world, including at the São Paulo Biennial, the Prague Biennale, Moderna Museet (Stockholm), and M HKA (Antwerp).

Ellinor Lager (b. 1986, Sweden) works with many different techniques and materials such as clay, metal, and textiles. Since 2019, she has also worked as a doula as part of her exploration of language and the experience of pregnancy and childbirth. She is educated at HDK-Valand, University of Gothenburg, and at Malmö Art Academy, and has worked as an assistant to the artist Theaster Gates in Chicago and at dOCUMENTA(13) in Kassel.

Gloria López Cleries (b. 1988, Spain) is a transdisciplinary artist, researcher, and lecturer with a background in art, art history, visual culture, and pedagogy. Her work critically examines issues of neoliberal rhetoric regarding emotional capitalism and new online models of productivity, affect, care, and collectivity. She is also a lecturer in fine art at HDK-Valand, University of Gothenburg.

Truls Melin (1958–2022, Sweden) drew inspiration from minimalism as well as surrealism and developed a style of his own characterized by a low-key poetic playfulness. His monochrome sculptures and installations made a significant impression on the Swedish art scene and, among other projects, he represented Sweden in the Nordic Pavilion at the 1993 Venice Biennale. Melin was educated at the Forum Art School in Malmö and the Royal Danish Academy of Fine Arts in Copenhagen.

Britt-Ingrid Persson BIP (b. 1938, Sweden) is a sculptor and ceramicist based in Stockholm. Using the signature BIP, she has since the 1960s worked with sculptural objects, mainly in unglazed clay, bronze, and concrete. The sculptures give shape to her ideas about the world, both politically and existentially. She is educated at Konstfack—University of Arts, Crafts and Design in Stockholm.

Iris Smeds (b. 1984, Sweden) is an artist whose work revolves around the marketability of the individual and examines our existence and society from a poetic and performative perspective. Her projects blur the boundaries between installation, performance, video, and sculpture. She has done numerous performances in Sweden and abroad, and her work has been shown at, among others, Moderna Museet (Stockholm), SixtyEight Art Institute (Copenhagen), and Bonniers Konsthall (Stockholm). Since 2013, she has also run the one-woman punk band Vaska Fimpen.

Superflex (Bjørnstjerne Christiansen, b. 1969; Jakob Fenger, b. 1968; Rasmus Rosengren Nielsen, b. 1969, Denmark) was founded in 1993 and works with art projects that have a direct impact on society. Through painting, public art, drinks, hypnosis sessions, and energy systems, the group has developed alternative models for social and economic organization.

Hannah Toticki (b. 1984, Denmark) works with sculpture, installation, and performance. Inspired by theater, design, and fashion, and mixed with humor, she connects the global and the personal and makes us aware of the body's relationship to economics and technology. She is educated at the Royal Danish Academy of Fine Arts in Copenhagen and has exhibited at, among others, the National Museum of Contemporary Art Athens (EMST), the Museum of Contemporary Art Detroit (MOCAD), and Galerie Wedding (Berlin).

Ulla Wiggen (b. 1942, Sweden) has worked as an artist since 1963. Until 1969, she produced a series of paintings depicting the interior of computers, such as circuit boards and electronics. After a 25-year hiatus, when she instead worked as a psychotherapist, she resumed working with art in 2013. Since then, she has mainly devoted herself to painting human internal organs, such as the brain and the iris of the eye. She has exhibited internationally, including at the Venice Biennale, Museum Tinguely (Basel), Centre Pompidou (Paris), Whitechapel Gallery (London), and New Museum (New York).

Colophon

Published in connection with the exhibition *Happily Ever After* at Malmö Konstmuseum (10.27.2023–03.31.2024)

Editors
Julia Björnberg
Anna Johansson

Authors
Nina Björk: pp. 14–17
Julia Björnberg: pp. 10–13, 20–107
Kirse Junge-Stevnsborg: p. 8
Anna Johansson: pp. 10–13, 20–107

Translation
Jennifer Hayashida

Proofreading
Anna Granqvist

Graphic Design
Andréason & Leibel

Font: Favorit by Dinamo
Paper: Munken Lynx Rough 300g (cover) and Munken Lynx 120g (insert) by Arctic

Image Credits
Anders Sune Berg: pp. 41–43, 53
Mattias Idunger: pp. 60–61
Pirje Mykkänen/Finnish National Gallery: p. 95
Samaneh Roghani: p. 81
Johanna Rylander: pp. 3, 38–39, 102–105
Bernhardt Strauss: pp. 44–45
Jenny Thornell: p. 101
Helene Toresdotter: pp. 4, 21–23, 28–31, 33, 35–37, 51, 67–69, 70, 72–73, 76–77, 96–99
All other images courtesy of the artists

BUS 2023
Muhammad Ali, Anita Christoffersson, Stina Ebers, Jenny Grönvall, Leif Holmstrand, Truls Melin, Britt-Ingrid Persson BIP, Superflex, Ulla Wiggen

Published and distributed by

MOUSSE PUBLISHING
Contrappunto s.r.l.
Via Pier Candido Decembrio 28
20137 Milan, Italy

Available through:

MILAN
Mousse Publishing
moussemagazine.it

NEW YORK
DAP | Distributed Art Publishers
artbook.com

DIJON
Les presses du réel
lespressesdureel.com

LONDON
Antenne Books
antennebooks.com

AMSTERDAM
Idea Books
ideabooks.nl

BERLIN
Motto
mottodistribution.com

FIRENZE
LibroCo
libroco.it

First edition: 2023
Printed in Sweden by ByWind
ISBN: 978-88-6749-605-1
€ 25 / $ 29.95

MALMÖ KONSTMUSEUM
Malmöhusvägen 6
211 18 Malmö, Sweden
malmo.se/konstmuseum

With generous support from Beckett-Fonden and Grosserer L.F. Foghts Fond.

MALMÖ KONSTMUSEUM

City of Malmö

REGION SKÅNE

BECKETT·FONDEN